WINDSURFING
BASIC AND FUNBOARD TECHNIQUES

ROGER JONES
WINDSURFING
BASIC AND FUNBOARD TECHNIQUES

HARPER & ROW, PUBLISHERS

SAN FRANCISCO

1817

Cambridge
Hagerstown
Philadelphia
New York

London
Mexico City
São Paulo
Sydney

ACKNOWLEDGMENTS

Text and photography: Roger Jones
Design: Roger Jones
Layout: Marilyn Bullivant-Davey
Text editor: Judith Chopra
Production: Roger Jones
Typesetting: Imprint
Equipment loaned by: Sail Free Marketing (Canadian Mistral distributor); Steve LeVine, Tackle Shack, Pinellas Park, Florida; Maui Sails/Neil Pryde; Vinta Sailboards; Wayler Boardsailing Canada Ltd; GS Sports Inc (US Wayler distributor)

Cover photo: Jill Boyer, photographed by John Severson

LC 84-47975
ISBN 0-06-250429-0

Printed and bound in Italy by Sagdos.   A Roger Jones Production

CONTENTS

THE WIND IS FREE II

This is a rewritten and rephotographed edition of *The Wind is Free*, or as it was called in America *Windsurfing with Ken Winner*. The original edition became something of a classic, selling over 150,000 English-language copies in four years and being published in seven other languages. Since the current edition doesn't involve boardsailor Winner we retitled the American edition *Windsurfing: Basic and Funboard Techniques*.

Chapters one to seven describe basic technique for long boards, including funboards which can be uphauled. Chapters eight to thirteen are for people learning high performance moves. Even beginners who expect never to ride big waves will find useful information in these later chapters, which are written to be accessible to beginners and intermediate sailors. I hope readers gain as much pleasure in reading the book as I did in creating it.

Good Sailing!
Roger Jones

PHOTO: ROSINA MAGUIRE

THE AUTHOR Roger Jones was born in Wales but spent his teens in Cornwall where he learned traditional surfing. Graduating in molecular sciences from the University of Warwick, he worked in publishing and in advertising before starting his own publishing company in 1973. His fiction, poetry, essays and articles on subjects as diverse as chemical engineering, film and social history, have appeared in periodicals in Britain, North America and Australia. Among many other interests he has presented features for the BBC, written and illustrated a series of walking/local history guides to Wales, and collected archival material on the subject of immigration into Canada. He began windsurfing in 1978 and divides his time between Hawaii and homes in Britain and Canada.

PREFACE

Roger called me one afternoon and asked if he could come by to discuss a project of his, a new book on windsurfing. He wanted to check certain details about the early days.

When we met and the full scope of the book became apparent, I realized how far the sport had come in the years since that day in 1967 when I taught myself to windsurf. Roger went further and reminded me of some prophetic words I wrote in 1969 to the effect that "it could be that there are still many useful maneuvers and techniques of greater difficulty which are as yet undiscovered," an understatement of the first magnitude as proved on the pages following. When I wrote that sentence, I really had no idea what youth and talent could do in expanding the dimensions of the sport. In fact, the sport itself, while acknowledging contributions by early pioneers, owes far more to its current legion of enthusiasts for their innovations and embellishments.

At the start the only purpose I had in mind was to create a sport which had the appeal of snow skiing, water skiing, surfing and sailing, but without their drawbacks. It was a lot like solving a complicated puzzle which had no rules except the laws of physics and which might or might not have a solution. Attempting such a puzzle doesn't attract everyone, but it does me. Indeed this is the sort of problem I've tackled for over 30 years in my profession as an aircraft designer.

I didn't think one way or the other about the sport's appeal beyond my circle of friends with similar athletic interests. I certainly didn't foresee the Europeans taking the lead in popularizing the sport and would hardly have predicted its overnight spread to the Eastern Bloc, Japan, Australia, South Africa and virtually every country blessed with some amount of wind, water and leisure. All of this has given me great pleasure, but the biggest surprise of all was its inclusion in the Olympic Games. I'm confident that boardsailing is now a permanent feature on the worldwide sports landscape and that its continued rapid growth foretells still more new and exciting developments.

Jim Drake
California

James R. Drake, inventor of the free-sail system

INTRODUCTION

CATCHING THE FEVER Windsurfing brings you into closer rapport with wind, water and your craft than any other sport because your body itself becomes part of the sailboard's mechanism.

Windsurfing fever is usually caught that first time you keep your balance for a few minutes, gliding across the water with a high worth all the preceding dunkings. If you aren't careful you can become so addicted that whenever the wind is up you drop whatever else you're doing and get out on your board.

As you put in more hours you learn to cope with higher winds. Then one day the moment comes when you're leaning back against a good 15-knot breeze, the rig held in perfect balance, the board skipping over the water, and suddenly it all feels gloriously effortless. You hardly know whether you're sailing, surfing or flying. You just know it feels so good you want to keep doing it forever.

It's a misconception that great strength is necessary. To rival the champions you'll certainly need to be fit. But from the statistic that over half those passing certified boardsailing courses are women you can tell that balance and technique are the keys to success, not brute strength. I should add that choosing a smaller sail for higher wind also helps a great deal.

To become an expert you'll need many hours of practice, but time on the water isn't enough in itself. Your time must be directed towards learning specific skills. You must have a clear understanding of the techniques you want to master. To achieve this, read books and magazines, watch experts, and don't be afraid to ask for advice. When you take up windsurfing you join a worldwide fraternity which, in my experience, readily accepts and helps you wherever you go.

FATHERS OF THE SPORT Two accounts of "sailboards" carrying hand-held sails were published in the United States during the mid-1960s. The first was by a Pennsylvania inventor named S. Newman Darby, the other by James R. Drake, a Southern Californian. Drake's paper *Wind Surfing – A New Concept in Sailing* was presented at the first American Institute for Aeronautics and Astronautics (AIAA) Technical Symposium on Sailboat Design in Los Angeles, on April 26th 1969, and published by the RAND corporation of Santa Monica, California. In his paper Drake described the development of windsurfing by himself and others, including Hoyle Schweitzer who later became the American manufacturer of Windsurfer brand boards and holder of a patent on the free-sail system.

Many people now claim to have developed sailboards prior to the Drake invention, and in each country where the patent was taken out distributors and manufacturers have gone to court to dispute the patent. In Britain, for example, one such dispute resulted in the court invalidating the patent there on the grounds of "obviousness." An interesting verdict.

S. Newman Darby's rather clumsy unpatented design was published in *Popular Science*, August 1965, in an article headed "Sailboarding: Exciting New Water Sport For High-Speed Water Fun . . . A Sport So New That Fewer Than 10 People Have Yet Mastered It." A square-rigger, Darby's sailboard was designed to be pushed by the wind. A limited number were sold around 1965 but the design didn't catch on. It was the success of the Drake/Schweitzer system which led to today's numerous types, sizes and brands.

Hoyle Schweitzer (middle) relaxes during a Windsurfer World Championships

With a simplicity in itself beautiful, the Drake/ Schweitzer system consists merely of a long slim hull with tail fin (skeg), universally-hinged mast, sail, wishbone boom, and a centerboard/daggerboard in a slot behind the mast. No mechanical devices, no pulleys or levers come between you and the elements. No shrouds support the rig. No rudder steers you. This is why boardsailing is so direct, why it differs so markedly from traditional sailing. The rider supports the sail by holding the boom, steers by tilting the rig and by exerting force on the hull with the feet.

Most of the problem-solving associated with the development was by Jim Drake, an aeronautics engineer whose many projects include contributions to the B70 supersonic strategic bomber and the Cruise missile. Drake reports that the concept grew out of conversations with his friend Fred Payne, a scientist, beginning in 1961. Drake also acknowledges development contributions by Allen Parducci (an anthropologist) and Hoyle Schweitzer.

The idea of an articulated mast, which led to the patent, was conceived by Jim while driving westbound, alone, on the San Bernadino Freeway. By early 1967 he was experimenting with two versions of a free-sail system, one with a fully-articulated universal on the mast foot, the other with the mast attached rigidly to the centerboard. The rigid connection made the centerboard swivel back as the mast was tilted forward. Both versions allowed the sail to swing in a full circle.

Drake decided to go with the fully-articulated universal. He and Schweitzer continued to experiment and in 1969 Drake reported that six different designs had been built and tested. These were given lighthearted names – for example,

Big Red, The Door, and Yellow submarine, "named because of its habit of sounding like a harpooned whale whenever the wind blew very strongly."

In 1968 patent processes were initiated in Britain, Germany, Australia, Canada, Japan and the USA, and a copyright was registered in the Netherlands. Schweitzer decided to go into business making the new craft and by 1970 he was producing a limited number of what he called Baja-Boards, made of plastic foam coated with fiberglass. In 1973 he bought out Jim Drake's share in the patent.

A tenacious man, Schweitzer – aided throughout by his wife Diane – was able to keep the sport slowly progressing out of obscurity. But because of limited promotion and marketing few people knew of windsurfing until 1973 when a Dutch textile manufacturer, Nijverdal Ten Cate, took a license to produce the Windsurfer in Europe. There the sport caught on like wildfire, particularly in Germany, the Netherlands and France. Dozens of companies began manufacturing (many pirating the patent) and in the five years from 1973 to 1978 about 150,000 sailboards were sold in Europe – 20 times more than were sold in North America during the sport's first decade.

Significant North American growth began in 1978, though interestingly per capita sales in Canada soon outstripped those in the USA. In the 1980s boardsailing's popularity has increased dramatically as more companies compete and promote the sport.

The acceptance of boardsailing into the 1984 Olympic Games was a tribute to the sport's unique qualities, in that other water sports of longer standing have repeatedly been denied Olympic status.

BASIC TECHNIQUE 1

*Jill Boyer at
Kahala, Honolulu,
photographed by
Darrell Wong*

SECTION ONE Long Boards

GETTING STARTED Boardsailing isn't difficult to learn in suitable conditions, and even your first wobbly attempts can be fun if you're properly prepared. This chapter will enable you to teach yourself basic balance and maneuvering in three to six hours and provide enough information for you to advance to intermediate level. You'll progress faster and more easily if you spread your initial learning over several sessions, giving yourself time to sleep on what you've learned.

Learn on calm water in light steady wind A shallow pond about a meter in depth and 100 to 200 meters across is ideal. This will be calm and you won't have far to walk back if (when) you fall prey to the "blown downwind syndrome" as all of us do at one time or another. Pick a place with steady wind that isn't disturbed by hills, tall buildings, trees, etc. A freaky wind whirling around obstacles makes sailing tricky.

It's dangerous to learn on a large expanse of water in offshore winds An offshore wind blows from land to water. When learning you inevitably drift with the wind and can end up far from land, unable to sail back. Be aware that offshore winds tend to increase as you get farther from land.

Avoid currents too. Be especially careful in tidal waters. You may set sail during slack tide (no current), then be carried out when the ebb starts. You can spot currents by the way water swirls around obstacles like posts and by the way moored boats all face the same way.

Stay close to land Select landmarks on shore as reference points. Check them frequently because you'll often lose track of time and circumstances when concentrating on sailing. Before you drift more than 100 meters from shore, kneel and paddle in. At first it's a good idea to tether the board to something on shore using about 30 meters of light line tied through the centerboard slot or around the centerboard under the sailboard. Then you can pull yourself ashore.

Wear a wetsuit or a drysuit Even in warm water I recommend you wear a wetsuit or a drysuit for protection against hypothermia. Hypothermia is a lowered deep body temperature which causes the body's vital functions to cease. This occurs more easily than many people realize. Prolonged immersion in water as warm as 20°C can cause loss of consciousness. Drysuits keep you warm by keeping water out. Wetsuits keep you warm by trapping a thin layer of water between your skin and the insulating neoprene of the suit. The neoprene also increases your buoyancy.

Stay with the board when in difficulty The board gives valuable flotation. By staying on it you'll be seen more easily by rescuers and will lose less body heat than you would in the water. If you can't sail, paddle the board ashore. Keep sail and board together. If they're separated, swim for the board first because it will quickly blow away, whereas the sail lies relatively stationary. To slow your drift downwind, remember that the sail lying in the water acts as a sea anchor. The deeper the sail lies, the more it slows your drift.

Identify wind direction before leaving shore You'll start sailing with your back to the wind and the board at right angles to the wind, so clearly distinguish wind direction by, for example, observing a flag or tossing something light into the air.

Learn self-rescue techniques If the wind dies or becomes too strong for you, or if your equipment breaks, you may have to paddle ashore. In flat water and light wind you can rest the boom on the back of the board, balanced to stop the sail dragging, then kneel or lie on the board and paddle with your hands or with the centerboard. If you can't make progress like this, unstep the mast, roll the sail, and lash it to the mast and boom with the outhaul and uphaul lines. Lay the rig lengthwise on the board and paddle using crawl or breaststroke. Derigging and paddling is difficult in rough conditions, so practice a few times. Withdraw the battens and, if your sail hasn't a special pocket for them on the mast tube, roll them tightly inside the sail. Roll the sail from clew to mast while supporting it on your outstretched legs.

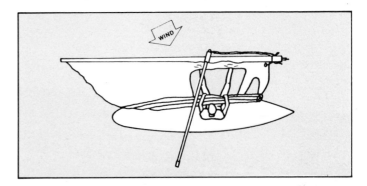

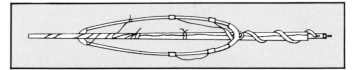

A buoyancy aid is a sensible precaution In some places "personal flotation devices" aren't merely recommended, they're mandatory. Choose one that isn't too bulky. I recommend a combined harness-buoyancy aid. A boardsailing harness has a hook in front which lines attached either side of the boom can loop into, so you can support the rig with your body weight.

BOARD AND RIG

1 Nose or bow.

2 Tail or stern.

3 Skeg or fin.

4 Daggerboard, or centerboard. Sometimes made to retract into the hull.

5 Footstraps.

6 Mast foot well or sliding mast track.

7 Mast.

8 Mast foot and universal joint.

9 Boom.

10 Sail clew.

11 Outhaul. Sometimes used with a pulley system, and tied off with a cleat on the boom.

12 Boom front end. Often with grip handle.

13 Inhaul. Tied off with a cleat.

14 Uphaul. Knotted to give grip.

15 Shock-cord.

16 Downhaul. Sometimes used with a pulley system, and tied off with a cleat on the mastfoot.

17 Safety cord. Joins the mastfoot to the board.

18 Battens. Fitted into batten pockets.

19 Leech of sail.

20 Foot of sail.

21 Luff of sail.

22 Mast sleeve.

23 Head of sail.

24 Tack of sail.

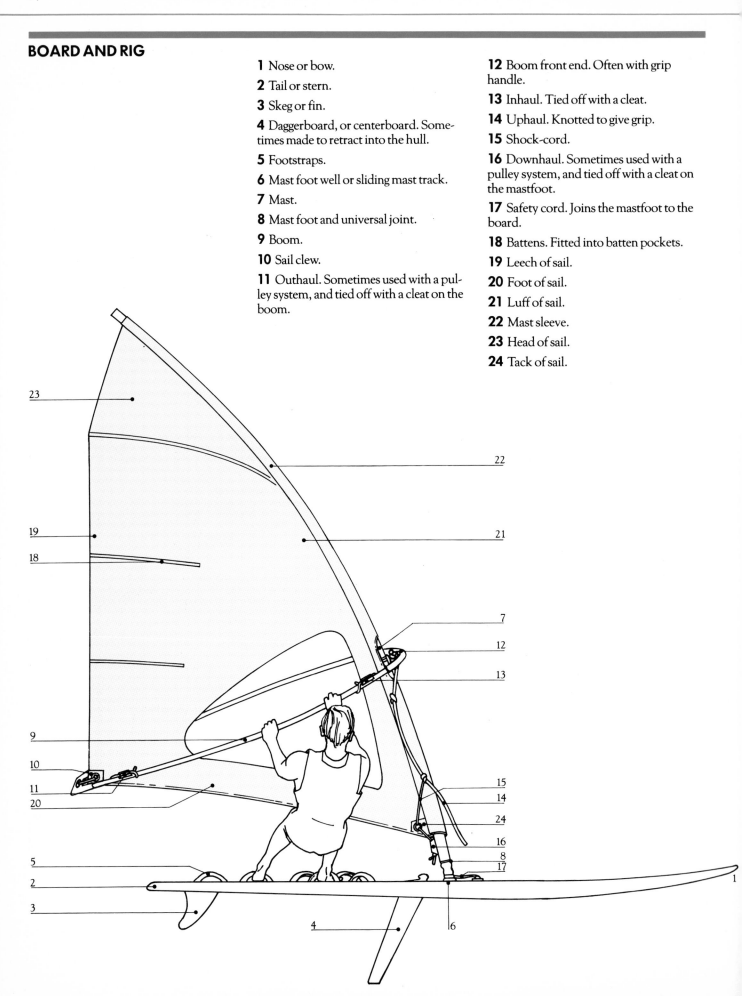

RIGGING Though each type of board differs slightly in the way it's assembled, these instructions are easily adapted.

1 Push the mast into the sail sleeve. If the sail has battens put them into the pockets sewn into the trailing edge, taking care to secure them so they can't slip out.

2 Slide the mastfoot into the mast, but first remove all sand and grit from both parts or you'll have great difficulty separating them.

3 Use the downhaul line to secure the mastfoot to the grommet in the lower front corner of the sail. If your equipment doesn't have a line or cleat attached to the mastfoot, tie the line to the slot on the mastfoot or around the sail grommet using the bowline knot illustrated in chapter two. Thread the line between the mastfoot and the sail, looping it a couple of times to give purchase, then tension the line and tie it off with two half hitches. Before tying it take a turn or two around the line, to take tension off the knot itself so it remains easy to untie.

4 Tie a figure-eight knot in one end of the inhaul. Secure the inhaul to the mast through the slot in the sail sleeve using one loop of a prusik hitch, as illustrated. Pull the knot tight against the loop, leaving the other end free. Stand the mast upright and position the inhaul so the boom will be at about shoulder height. As your own style develops, you'll find what height best suits you.

5 Pass the uphaul (thickest rope) through the hole in the front of the boom and tie a figure-eight knot in the top to retain it. Some people tie two or three equally spaced knots in the remainder for handholds.

6 Secure the boom tightly to the mast by passing the inhaul down through one hole in the boom, once around the mast, up through the other hole, then through the cleat. The boom must be snug enough not to move when you sail or you'll lack precision. The best way to achieve this is to lie the mast on the ground, boom on top, uphaul down, then slip the top of the mast inside the boom. Next thread the inhaul line through the boom end as already described and pull it tight. After cleating the line I usually use a retaining knot to prevent slippage. Now when you raise the mast and scissor the boom down into operating position, the slack is taken up. Don't make the line so tight when the boom lies parallel to the mast that you crack the mast when the boom is swung down.

7 Cleat the outhaul line on one side of the boom. Pass the other end through the hole in the boom end, through the grommet in the back (clew) of the sail, back through the other hole in the boom end, and along the boom to the other cleat. Tighten the line until the sail has good shape, then cleat it. A knot at the cleat prevents slippage. There's more on correct sail tensioning in chapter two. Note that funboard sails, those with plump or fatheads, require more tension than traditional pinhead sails.

8 To keep the uphaul within reach connect it to the mastfoot or to the downhaul with a short piece of elastic cord. Push the mastfoot into the appropriate slot in the board and, for added security, connect the rig to the board with the safety leash. (Rig = mast-sail-boom-mastfoot unit.) If the board has two mast sockets use the forward position when learning, unless you find this makes the nose dig under waves. With a sliding mast track use a mid position. (However, whenever you're having trouble because strong wind is turning the board towards the wind, positioning the mast further forward eases this.)

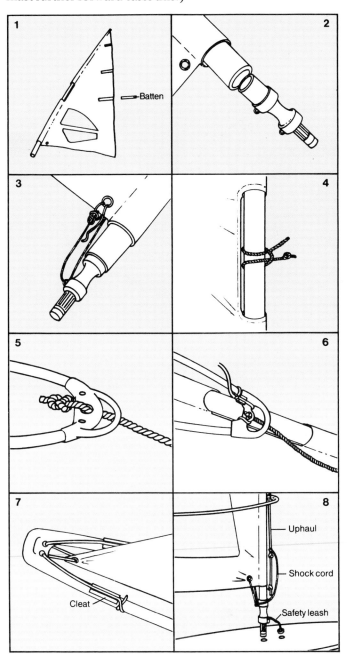

LAND TRAINING A brief session of land training is useful to accustom your body to the motions of raising the sail, foot placement and correct sail handling. A simulator helps. This consists of a stand and a cutdown sailboard which pivots around the daggerboard as you incline the sail, much as a board turns on the water. You can make do by placing your board on the ground with its skeg removed or buried. To practice the startup procedure arrange the board at right angles to the wind. Move it head-to-wind to practice tacking.

RAISING THE SAIL Kelby Anno demonstrates land practice. Precisely the same technique is used when on water.

Arrange the board in the water at right angles to the wind, with the sail lying in the water on the side farthest from the wind (leeward side). The sail should make a right angle with the board.

Locate the midline, an imaginary line running along the middle of the board from nose to tail. Make a habit of keeping your weight over the midline to avoid capsizing. Now, keep the board at right angles to the wind and your back to the wind, and climb on.

Stand with the arches of your feet on the board's midline, feet shoulder width apart either side of the mastfoot. Hold the uphaul rope in one hand, leaving the other arm free to aid balance. Don't pull the sail up immediately: first get the feel of the board by rocking it from side to side with your ankles. You'll balance better if you keep hips, knees and ankles flexible. People automatically tend to tense on feeling the board rock, but tensing only decreases stability.

To lift the sail, first squat down and pull the uphaul taut. Then lean back slightly and straighten your knees to let your thighs take most of the strain. Don't try to lift the sail all in one go. Lift just enough for some of the water to run

off. Keep your bottom in, back straight, and lift with thighs, arms and body weight, not with your back. Maintain the board at right angles to the wind and your back to the wind.

The rig lightens as water runs out of the mast sleeve. At this point pull the uphaul in steadily, hand over hand, until the sail is entirely clear of the water. The sail lifts more easily if you pull the mast very slightly towards the wind to create an airflow under the fabric.

With the sail clear of the water, hold the uphaul near the boom and allow the sail to align itself downwind, flapping loosely like a flag (luffing). Keep the end of the sail out of the water, otherwise it'll fill with wind and be jerked out of your hands or pull you off.

If the sail is in the water on the upwind (windward) side you can pull it to the other side by dragging the mast across the back of the board (the boom tends to jam on the nose) while stepping around with small steps.

As your skill increases, try lifting the sail from the windward side without first dragging it around. Pull it quickly out of the water with the mast pointing directly into the wind, then let it blow around while you spin and lean back on the uphaul to counterbalance it. You'll have to be quick deciding which way the sail is going to spin or it'll knock you off.

LAUNCHING To avoid scratching my equipment by dragging it I usually carry a long board and rig separately to the water's edge. (A short board can be carried overhead with rig attached, as shown in Chapter 9.) Carry the sail overhead, mast perpendicular to the wind or aligned with it so you fly the sail.

To launch, hold the mast in your windward hand and the skeg or footstrap in the other, and push the board into the water nose first. When you lower the tail to the water you'll be in the right position to simply step on and set sail. It's easier to keep the board perpendicular to waves if you push it in on edge. For launching in shorebreak see Chapter 11.

When launching in a situation requiring rig and board be

put into the water separately, place the rig flat on the water first, because it won't drift far. Don't place the hull on the water first, then go for the rig, because a hull quickly drifts away.

1   2   3

4   5   6

TURNING THE BOARD Learn to turn the board around beneath yourself by holding the uphaul, the sail flapping loosely in front of you, and tilting the sail towards the front or the back of the board. Whichever way you tilt the sail the board turns the opposite way.

Lean the mast towards the front of the board in a sweeping motion, pushing away with your front foot, and the nose turns away from the wind (bears off). To turn the board the other way (head up), lean the sail towards the back and push with your back foot. At this stage don't be concerned whether you're bearing off or heading up. Just concentrate on turning one way then the other.

The board responds best when the sail is held slightly away from your body, so hold the uphaul close to the boom and extend your arms. Bend your knees slightly and counterbalance the weight of the rig with that of your upper body. Take care not to dip the end of the sail or the boom in the water. As the board turns, keep your back to the wind and the sail in front of you by walking around the mast in small steps. Keep your feet close to the mast so as not to tip the board, and avoid tensing those legs and hips when the board wobbles!

Until you learn more efficient turning methods this is how you'll turn the board when you've sailed away from shore and want to turn and sail back. Practice turning the board completely around in both directions.

1

2

THE START-UP SEQUENCE To get underway you must perform a special starting sequence.

1 Keeping your back to the wind, hold the uphaul and tilt the mast forward or back as necessary to align the board at right angles to the wind, so you end up with the sail fluttering out downwind at right angles to the board. Hold the uphaul near the boom, keeping the boom end out of the water.

Place your forward foot in front of and touching the mast step and place your back foot on about the middle of the centerboard case, feet shoulder-width apart.

2 Keeping the sail empty of wind (luffing), cross your front hand over your back hand and grasp the boom 12 to 25 inches from the mast.

3 In one smooth motion, turn your body and front foot slightly towards the nose of the board as the front hand leans the mast towards the nose of the board, past your front shoulder, and slightly towards the wind. As you do this your back hand releases the uphaul and prepares to grasp the boom about shoulder width from the front hand. Keep your body upright, back straight and slightly hollow.

4 Grasp the boom with your back hand and pull the back of the sail towards you enough to completely fill the sail. (This is called sheeting in.) At the same time rake the mast slightly farther towards the front of the board and drive the board forward with your front foot. Keep that back straight and slightly hollow, and your bottom in. Don't let the sail lean away from you or pull you forward at the waist.

5 Once the board is moving, bring the mast back almost to the vertical so you sail off in a more or less straight line. If you leave the mast angled forward too much the board will turn downwind.

In light wind, stand upright with your knees slightly bent. As the wind strengthens, lean back to counterbalance the sail. Find a comfortable position for your feet. Both feet are usually behind the mast when on a steady course.

3

SAIL CONTROL Your back hand controls the sail's power. Pulling in increases power until you pull in so far that you stall the sail. Letting the sail out (sheeting out) reduces power. While sailing, glance at the sail occasionally to see that you're sheeting in just enough to fill the sail and no further.

You'll avoid some spills if you practice sheeting in and out on land. In particular, avoid leaning forward at the waist, and avoid letting the sail lean away to leeward. Such positions make it difficult for you to sheet out without overbalancing, thus increasing the likelihood of your being overpowered. The golden rule is to keep the mast upright, or in stronger wind incline it slightly over you, towards the wind.

STANCE When sailing upwind in light air aim to stand upright with your back slightly hollow, both arms bent, hands close together. Position your feet over or close to the centerboard.

React to fluctuations in wind speed and direction by sheeting in and out and by adjustments of the knees, hips and waist, using your upper body and bottom as counterweights.

4

Stance for sailing close-hauled in light air

STEERING Put simply, you steer by raking the mast towards the front or the back of the board. Rake the mast forward and sheet in, and the front turns away from the wind. Rake the mast back and sheet in and you turn towards the wind.

More accurately, you lean the sail not directly towards the nose or tail but in the direction of the sail's chord line, which is a line joining the front and back boom ends.

Heading up Turning the board towards the wind is called heading up. To head up, rake the mast towards the back of the board and pull the sail in with the back hand while shifting weight onto your back foot.

The board heads up more sharply if you do any of the following: lean the rig further back; bank the leeward rail (edge) of the board down with the back foot; sheet in harder.

Turn away from the wind by leaning the mast forward and to windward

STOPPING At first the simplest way to stop is by dropping the sail and pushing it down in the water. Once your balance improves, stop by backing the sail: put your forward hand on the mast below the boom and push out with your back hand to fill the sail on the other side. This will bring you rapidly to a halt.

Turn towards the wind by raking the mast back

Bearing off Turning downwind is called bearing off or bearing away. To bear away, lean the mast forward and sheet in slightly while pushing the nose away from the wind with your front foot.

As the board turns, the angle the sail makes with the wind alters. Hence, once the board begins turning downwind, ease the sail out slightly with your back hand to maintain the most efficient sheeting angle.

FALLING You may think falling will come naturally, and the least said, the better. But if you understand the common kinds of fall and how to avoid them, you'll learn to stay up more quickly and easily.

Most spectacular is the catapult fall where the lucky sailor is pulled forward and flung through the air, landing some distance ahead of the board. Beginners rarely catapult because this occurs in strong wind, often while bearing away.

Gusts On the other hand it is common for beginners to be pulled forward by gusts. When this happens, sheet out, pushing the sail away with the back hand to spill air. Once pressure is released, use the front hand to pull the mast upright again, or even rake the mast slightly towards the wind before you sheet in again. If the gust is severe, rather than fall, let go entirely with your back hand (or even with both hands if doing so will save you from falling), crouch down quickly and grab the uphaul or the bottom of the mast; grab anything that will stop you falling off the board.

Avoid letting the sail lean away from you

Lulls Another kind of fall occurs when you're dropped backwards by a sudden lull. In this case, arrest your fall by crouching quickly and sheeting in with your back hand to gain extra force from the sail.

Backwinding You can also be knocked backwards when the wind fills the sail from the other side, slamming you into the water. This can happen when you're sailing too close to the wind, the wind is shifty, or a gust causes the board to head up suddenly. When a gust hits, you must lean the mast to windward and forward to avoid heading up.

Balance Balance is generally easier if you keep your weight low. Some courses are tougher to balance on than others. A close reach is easiest. A broad reach and a run in choppy water are hardest.

TACKING AND GYBING A course change in which the nose of the board turns towards and then through the eye of the wind is a *tack*. (The eye of the wind is the direction from which the wind blows.) The opposite kind of turn, in which the nose turns downwind so that the tail points into the wind as you pass through the eye of the wind, is a *gybe*.

At first you can tack and gybe by releasing the boom, grasping the uphaul, and walking the board around as already described in the section entitled "Turning the Board." This leaves you vulnerable to being knocked off, however, so give priority to learning the faster, more efficient tacks and gybes described on the following pages.

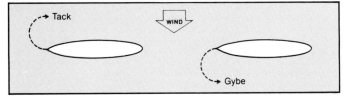

Figure 1

CHOOSING YOUR COURSE In keeping with the rest of this chapter, the information here is basic, intended for those new to sailing.

The diagrams show the various courses, named according to their orientation to the wind. Note that the angle of the sail to the wind changes very little, but the angle the sail makes with the hull changes greatly.

Here are some tips on sailing various courses. Learn to be sensitive to the direction the wind is coming from. Bear in mind that as your sailing speed changes, the velocity and direction of the wind you actually feel will change, since the wind created by your forward motion interacts with the true wind.

Close reach Beginners find a close reach an easy point of sail. Balance is easy, as is maintaining a course. Figure 2 shows the approximate angle of the sail to the wind and to the board on this and the other principal courses. Practice a close reach first, since each time you fall you'll drift downwind and this will enable you to gain ground upwind.

Beating Because it's impossible to sail directly into the wind you must gain ground upwind by beating – that is, by sailing upwind on alternate tacks (figure 3). You progress most effectively upwind by sailing close-hauled. Your speed is relatively slow on this heading, so sail patiently and carefully. Tack quickly, and resume the close-hauled course as soon as possible, or you'll drift downwind again.

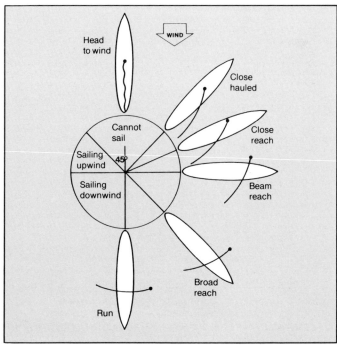

Figure 2 Sail trim for various courses

Running Sailing directly with the wind is known as running. To get onto a run, tilt the mast radically forward and to windward, then sheet in. As the board turns downwind, sheet out and turn your body forward, shifting your feet till they're either side of the centerboard well.

When pointing directly downwind, sheet out fully so that the sail is at right angles to the board, and lean the mast so the mid-point of the sail is over the midline of the board. Look ahead through the window. Steer by tilting the sail to left or right rather than towards front or back as you did when close-hauled. Tilting the sail to the right makes the board turn left, and vice versa.

Rough water makes balance difficult on a run. If shaky, bend your knees and place one foot ahead of the other, heels turned in slightly so you can respond to the rocking of the board by bending your ankles.

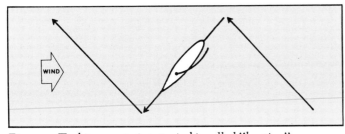

Figure 3 Tacking to a point upwind is called "beating"

Close-hauled The close-hauled stance in light air is illustrated on page 21. When close-hauled, the mast is held upright and close to the body. The rear boom end is over the downwind corner of the board and the sail should be just on the verge of luffing. (A sail is said to luff when the front part flaps and looks as if the wind is pushing it from the other side, instead of being full and curving smoothly from the mast to the trailing edge.)

Check that your sail is efficiently set by sheeting out till you see it luff. Then sheet in just enough to see and feel the wind fill the entire sail.

FAST TACKING The key to fast tacking is to sail the board around. Keep the sail sheeted in on the original tack until the bow passes through the wind, then step or jump quickly around the mast to the new side, throw the mast forward and sheet in on the new tack.

You need to be ready for rough conditions, perhaps also for competition, so practice the identical set of movements until you perform swiftly and surely every time. Don't expect to master a lightning-fast tack immediately. First practice at your own pace on flat water, in moderate steady wind. Once you have the movements and timing down pat, then start to increase your speed.

Marina Lari demonstrates.

1 Head up by leaning the sail back strongly, pulling in with your back hand and weighting your back foot. To head up faster in lighter wind, bank the leeward edge of the board down slightly with the back foot.

2 As you approach the eye of the wind, place your front foot directly in front of the mast step and your front hand on the mast below the boom. In this position you're ready to jump around the mast at the next stage, yet you can continue sailing the board around until head-to-wind.

When racing, particularly in light and moderate wind, don't pull the sail in any further than the board's centerline or you'll lose forward speed unnecessarily. However, when it's probable you'll be knocked off if you haven't got a full sail to hang onto, it may be necessary to pull the bow entirely through the wind, onto the new tack, before jumping around to the new side.

3 & 4 With the board passing through the eye of the wind, release the boom entirely and step in front of the mast, passing the mast from hand to hand. Keep your legs slightly bent, your stance solid, and place your feet firmly. For a really fast tack, pass through this position in the merest fraction of a second as you step or jump to the new side, throwing the mast forward with the new front hand. In strong wind, two hands may be needed to throw the mast forward. There's a knack of counterbalancing the sail's inertia as you throw it forward, with that of your body as you jump back, which unites both movements into one clean action.

5 With both hands on the boom, lean the mast forward.

6 Sheet in and push the nose off the wind with the front foot, giving the sail two or three pumps to accelerate.

1

4

2

3

5

6

Canada's Steve Jarrett performs a fast tack

GYBING There are many varieties of gybe. The type you perform depends on factors such as tightness of turn required, wind and water conditions, and your equipment.

Running gybe The basic running gybe is suitable for light wind.

Sail on a beam reach. Lean the sail forward and to windward, and start the board turning downwind by sheeting in for extra power. Let the sail out as the board turns. When you're headed dead downwind, continue leaning the sail over the side and scoop the wind to pull the tail around, through the eye of the wind.

Once through the eye of the wind, release the back hand from the boom, allowing the sail to swing around. Grasp the mast with your free hand and pull it across to the other side of the board as the sail swings, so that by the time the sail reaches the new side the mast is positioned ready for sheeting in. Grasp the boom with the new back hand, then the front hand, and sheet in.

1

2

4

5

3

6

Advanced gybe When you've gained some experience, try this technique. The account begins at a beam reach heading.

1 Move your feet to behind the centerboard, placing one near each rail. Keep your weight evenly distributed over both feet and crouch for added stability. Lean the sail forward and to windward and initiate the turn by sheeting in and pushing the windward rail down with one foot, using the other foot to stop the lee rail tipping up too far.

2 & 3 Keep the sail near its luffing point as you turn, to reduce the chances of being pulled over. To bear off faster, pull the tail around with your feet.

4 Level the board off as you approach a run. Pull the tail through the eye of the wind by drawing the sail towards the tail, keeping it efficiently trimmed, while pushing the tail around with your feet.

5 Once past the eye of the wind you can release with your back hand, letting the sail flip around. In rough water and in gusty wind it's sometimes safer to delay flipping the sail until you've turned upwind slightly on the new tack.

6 As you let the sail flip, keep the mast raked back so the momentum doesn't pull it from your grip. At the same time pull the mast across your chest and over the other side of the board (towards the wind), then sheet in on the new tack.

The board turns more sharply if you step back sufficiently to raise the nose from the water. Step back far enough to stall the board's forward motion, and you can turn on a penny.

Marina Lari leans the mast back as she prepares to let the sail flip around for a gybe

2

USEFUL
INFORMATION

SAIL ADJUSTMENT

Sail adjustment isn't critical unless you're racing or sailing at very high speed in surf or in speed trials and the like. It's sufficient to adjust outhaul and downhaul tension till you achieve a clean aerofoil shape that doesn't bag out over the boom and has no folds or major wrinkles.

Outhaul and downhaul tensions must balance each other. The tighter the outhaul, the flatter the sail becomes. Here are a few hints.

- Sail bags out over boom – outhaul too lose.
- Wrinkles extend from clew – outhaul too tight.
- Vertical folds or wrinkles alongside mast – too much downhaul tension relative to outhaul. Loosen downhaul or tighten outhaul.
- Horizontal wrinkles or folds in mast sleeve and luff – downhaul too loose.

When you're new to the sport you'll find a fairly flat sail easier to control. Later, apply this very approximate rule: in lighter wind get maximum power by using a fuller sail; as the wind increases, flatten the sail by increasing outhaul and downhaul tension.

An exception to this is wind so light it can't fill the sail properly. In this case flatten the sail to make it more efficient and easier to pump. Another exception occurs in wind so strong you're overpowered. Then it sometimes helps to make the sail very full, because a full sail is easier to luff partially than a flat sail.

MAST TRACKS AND RETRACTABLE CENTERBOARDS

Many all-round funboards have sliding mast tracks and centerboards which retract into the hull. When you're getting used to the track, position the mast in the middle. Once you're used to tacking, bearing off and gybing, follow these guidelines, keeping an open mind for what feels most comfortable and works best.

When planing

Sailing upwind: mast fully forward; centerboard fully down or, if sailboard railing (tipping up), pulled up slightly.

Reaching: mast back, centerboard retracted.

Not planing

Sailing upwind: mast all or partway forward, depending on distance from nose (sometimes with the mast fully forward the board wanders off a close-hauled course); centerboard fully down.

Reaching: mast partway back; centerboard retracted or, to gain distance upwind, partially down.

Marginal planing conditions

Don't slide the mast all the way back in marginal conditions because moving your weight back delays planing and causes the board to drop off the plane sooner.

Reasoning The purpose of a mast track is to allow the sail to be kept upright while moving its center of effort forward or back to balance the board's center of resistance.

For sailing upwind you need a long wetted surface. This means keeping your weight forward and hence the mast positioned forward.

When you start planing on a reach you move your weight back and the front of the board planes out of the water. This and the fact that the centerboard is retracted moves the sailboard's center of lateral resistance back. To keep the sail's center of effort in balance with the center of lateral resistance, the sail must either be raked back or moved back. Raking the sail away from vertical reduces its efficiency – hence the mast track.

Here are some additional hints from World Cup racer Alex Aguera: "When sailing to windward in light wind and flat water I'd probably put my mast all the way forward, as long as it felt comfortable, because I do think it's faster forward. But sometimes, especially in choppy seas, it's necessary to move the mast back slightly to keep your speed up and the nose off the water. If you have to do a 720° penalty turn, bear in mind that it's much easier with the track all the way back."

RULES OF THE ROAD All boats, especially those in crowded waterways, must abide by the right-of-way rules.

Rule 1 Yours is probably the smallest boat on the water, and you're probably the least protected, so regardless of who has right-of-way, you'll come off worst in any collision. Hence rule 1: avoid collision and the risk of collision.

Rule 2 When two sailboats meet on opposite tacks, the one on port tack shall give way. Since the right hand is forward when on starboard, I remember this as "Right hand forward has right of way."

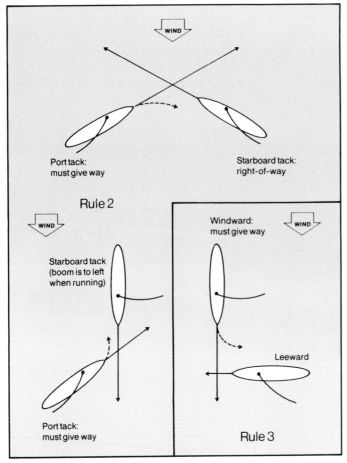

Port tack:
must give way

Starboard tack:
right-of-way

Rule 2

Starboard tack
(boom is to left
when running)

Windward:
must give way

Leeward

Port tack:
must give way

Rule 3

Rule 3 When two sailboats meet on the same tack, the boat to windward must give way.

Rule 4 When one boat is overtaking another, the overtaking boat shall keep clear.

Rule 5 A boat that is obstructed by other right-of-way boats or by the shore may demand room to navigate around the obstruction.

Rule 6 When a sailboat and powerboat meet, the more maneuverable boat must give way – that is, don't demand rights from a supertanker.

You share the water with swimmers, so be especially careful to watch for them. If you run over someone you'll very likely cause serious injury.

SAFETY Check the weather report before you go sailing and keep an eye on the sky while out. Try to be aware of how conditions may change. Read a book on weather and learn to recognize when squalls and storms are approaching. When there's danger of lightning get to shore and away from the mast, or if you can't get to shore then stop sailing and push the mast down into the water until the storm has passed.

In wind so strong you can't sail there are a number of alternatives.

1 Reef the sail by undoing the downhaul, pushing the sail up the mast to the boom, and tying it up there with the downhaul.

2 An onshore wind will blow you ashore if you stand holding the uphaul, letting the sail flap in front of you like a flag. If you can't lift the sail entirely lift it partially. In wind blowing more or less parallel to the shore you can get ashore by holding the uphaul with part of the sail dragging in the water. The sail will propel you across the wind.

3 When all else fails, de-rig and paddle diagonally across the waves, wind and/or current. If you can't make progress with the rig aboard, consider leaving it and paddling just the board. This depends on your chances of reaching land. Sometimes it may be better to rig the sail again, so you're more easily spotted by searchers.

4 To summon help let off a red flare (which you can keep inside the mast) or wave with both hands.

5 Another boardsailor can give you a ride or tow you. Tie the line to his mast base or hang onto it, having first removed or retracted your centerboard.

USEFUL KNOTS

Bowline This forms a loop that won't slip and is easy to untie. It's useful for tying the downhaul to the sail or to the mastfoot.

Two half hitches Two half hitches will secure a line to almost anything, and are often used to finish off the downhaul.

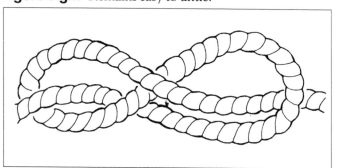

Figure eight Remains easy to untie.

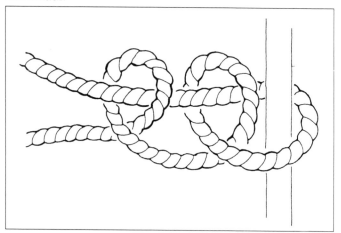

Overhand Can become impossible to untie.

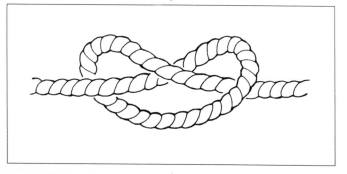

Prusik hitch Excellent for tying an inhaul to the mast.

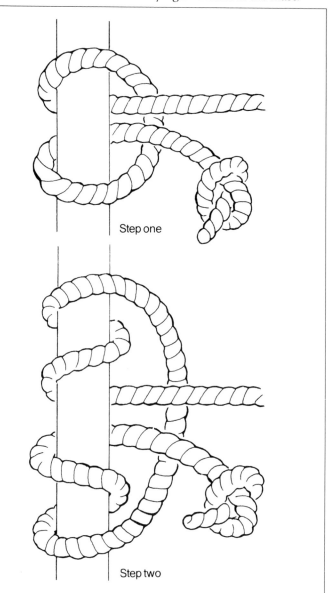

Step one

Step two

Trucker's hitch This type of trucker's hitch is easy to tie and untie and allows you to pull down on the board tightly enough to keep it on the roof rack no matter how strong the wind. (Keeping the rack on your car is another matter.)

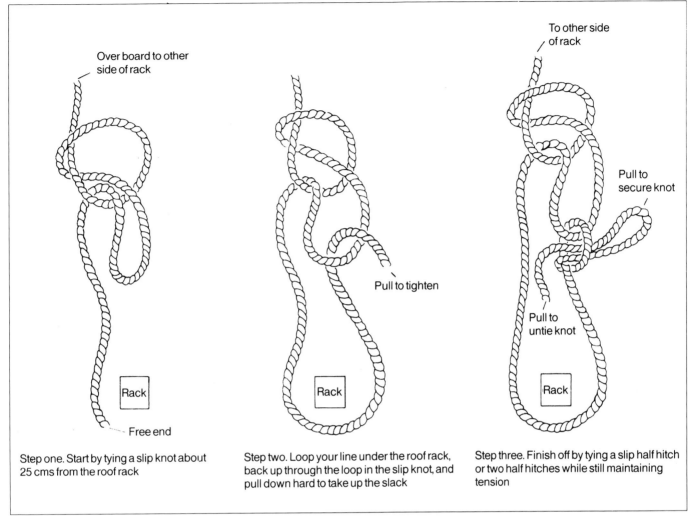

Over board to other
side of rack

Free end

Rack

Step one. Start by tying a slip knot about
25 cms from the roof rack

Pull to tighten

Rack

Step two. Loop your line under the roof rack,
back up through the loop in the slip knot, and
pull down hard to take up the slack

To other side
of rack

Pull to
secure knot

Pull to
untie knot

Rack

Step three. Finish off by tying a slip half hitch
or two half hitches while still maintaining
tension

3

BASIC THEORY

From left to right:
Mark Shields,
Lance Sprackman,
Kees Steenman

AIR FLOW
Understanding some basic theory generally helps you learn more rapidly.

The sail functions much like the wing of a plane. Air flows over the surface of a wing and generates an upward force known as *lift*. Similarly, air flowing past the sail generates lift, but in a horizontal direction.

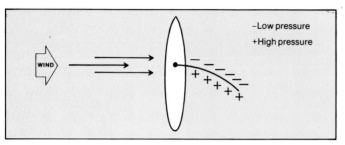

Figure 1

Upon meeting the sail the air flow is separated to pass either side. Air flowing past the leeward side is accelerated by the sail's curve, causing a reduction of air pressure. The greater pressure on the windward side then pushes the sail towards this lower-pressure area of the leeward side – that is, it produces lift (figure 1). This lift is generated roughly perpendicular to a line drawn from the mast to the clew (figure 2).

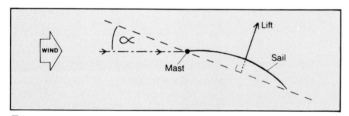

Figure 2

To use your sail efficiently, hold it at just the right angle (α) to the wind. This angle depends upon factors such as your point of sail. If the sail is held at too small an angle to the wind it luffs, and consequently part of its area is not used to generate force (figure 3).

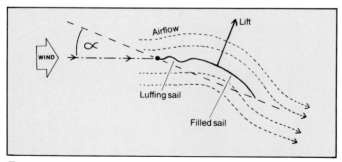

Figure 3

If the sail is at too great an angle to the wind it stalls (figure 4). Air can't flow smoothly past the leeward surface, but breaks up into swirls and eddies. There is no longer a reduction of pressure on the leeward side, so less overall driving force is generated. In fact, the wind mostly pushes the sail along, just as it does when you sail dead downwind.

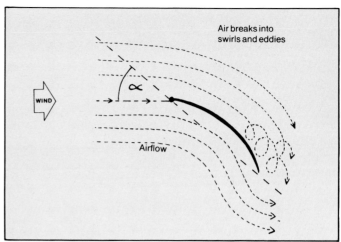

Figure 4

Between these two limiting angles of luff and stall there is a range of efficient sail lift generation. You can find this subject discussed in more detail in books on general sailing theory.

To improve your sailing ability you need to become sensitive to the balance of the boom. The center of effort (CE) of the sail is the point through which all the aerodynamic forces acting on the sail may be imagined to act. When a sail luffs a little, this CE moves aft (figure 5), putting more pressure on your back hand, and tending to turn the board towards the wind. Luffing has the same effect as raking the sail back. Involuntary luffing caused by strong gusts often causes beginners problems by turning them head-to-wind.

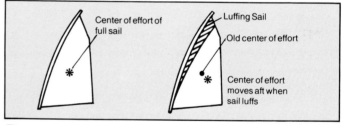

Figure 5

When the sail stalls the opposite happens: the CE moves forward, but in a far less pronounced way. Sensitivity to these variations will enable you to trim the sail more accurately and sail more efficiently.

BALANCE POINT OF THE BOOM
When you sail with your hands on the boom and an equal pull on each, the balance point is midway between them. Edge them closer and closer, and you can identify the precise position of the balance point – in light winds it's possible to hold the boom with one hand, or even a single finger. Practicing this improves rig control and sensitivity.

Holding on one-handed, a slight change in wind direction will cause the boom to swing one way or the other. A header causes it to swing towards you while a lift causes it to swing away. This isn't the way to spot the windshifts – but it is a useful experiment when you're learning.

The balance point of the boom alters with changes in wind strength and direction, when a gust bends the mast, or when the sail is improperly trimmed.

STEERING When we tilt the sail forward we move the CE ahead of the CLR, so that the board bears off the wind. Similarly, when we tilt the sail back, we move the CE aft of the CLR, so that the board heads up (figure 6).

However, when you're sailing downwind the force on the sail is in a forward direction and the resistance is directly opposed to this force. To steer, therefore, tilt the sail from side to side instead of forward and back (figure 7).

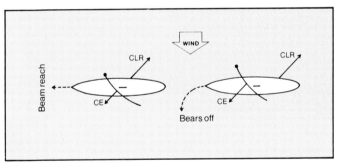

Figure 7 When running, steer by tilting the sail from side to side

From the previous two examples you can see why, when you're on a beam reach and wish to bear off to a broad reach, you tilt the mast slightly forward but mainly to windward (figure 8).

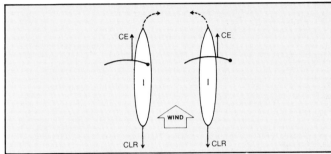

Figure 8

CENTERBOARD Much of the force generated by the sail is in a sideways direction, particularly when close-hauled. Since we don't want to go sideways, we use a centerboard. This is shaped to move through the water readily in a forward direction, but not easily sideways.

Just as the center of effort (CE) of a sail is the point through which you can imagine the forces on the sail to act, the center of lateral resistance (CLR) is the point through which you can imagine the resistance to sideways motion to act.

When sailing close-hauled the CLR is a point on the centerboard through which sideways forces act to balance the sideways component of the forces acting through the CE.

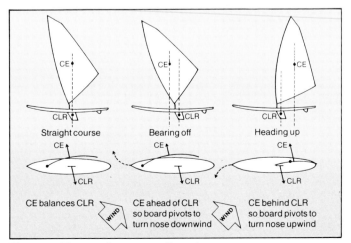

Figure 6 Turning forces on sailboard

PLANING Most sailboats move through the water. They push water aside as they pass. But some light-displacement boats, such as sailboards, are capable of skimming over the surface of the water – planing.

In light winds sailboards move at slower speeds and push through the water. But once the wind reaches 10 to 12 knots they can go fast enough to rise to the surface of the water and plane. The difference in speed between planing and almost planing is surprisingly great; that's why your first success in 12 knots of wind is so exciting.

APPARENT WIND The wind perceived by the sailor is known as the *apparent wind*. It is the vector combination of:
1 The *true wind* as observed by a stationary observer, and
2 The *induced wind* caused by the motion of the boat (which motion is also as perceived by a stationary observer). This induced wind is of equal speed but opposite direction to boat speed.

Consider the example of a true wind from the north at 8 Km/h, while you sail east at a speed of 6 Km/h: you will feel an apparent wind that is a vector combination of the true wind (8 Km/h, northerly) and the induced wind caused by your motion (6 Km/h, easterly). Substitute these values in the vector diagram (figure 9) and we have a right-angled triangle whose hypotenuse represents the value of the apparent wind. We can thus calculate the apparent wind as 10 Km/h from approximately the northeast.

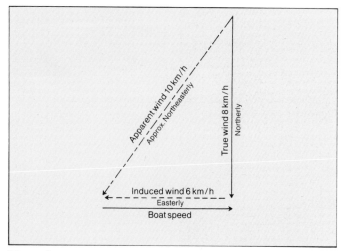

Figure 9

In other words, in this example the wind to which you trim your sail when you start from a stationary position is the 8 Km/h wind from the north. You then accelerate to a steady-state speed of 6 Km/h, at which time your sail should be trimmed to the 10 Km/h apparent wind from approximately northeast.

High-speed craft like sandyachts, iceboats, catamarans and sailboards can use this increase in apparent wind speed to travel faster than the true wind. The faster they go, the stronger their apparent wind; the stronger their apparent wind, the faster they go. This progression doesn't go on forever: eventually the apparent wind is brought so close to head-on that the sail is unable to produce still more driving force.

KEEPING WARM Hypothermia – a lowered deep body temperature – is one of the boardsailor's most dangerous enemies. Falls into cold water and exposure to chill winds can rapidly lower your body temperature and, as mentioned in chapter 1, prolonged immersion in water as warm as 20°C (68°F) can cause loss of consciousness. Bear this in mind and if you're sailing and find yourself shivering uncontrollably, go ashore and warm up before your body temperature drops to a point where heat loss becomes difficult to reverse without medical attention.

When deciding what to wear, bear in mind that it's generally colder on water than on land, and that conditions may change. Take into account air and water temperature, wind-chill factor, and how often you're likely to fall in.

WETSUITS Many boardsailors find their needs are met by a combination of longjohn wetsuit and jacket. A jacket with close-fitting neoprene body and loose fabric sleeves is popular because this keeps wind off the arms while not restricting circulation. Avoid tight wrist bands because these can impair your grip.

In the tropics a shortie wetsuit or neoprene vest often suffices.

Alex Aguera hamming it up for the camera in a shortie wetsuit

COLDER WEATHER GEAR

Drysuits When air and water get really chilly a drysuit may be the answer. A variety of different types are available, some of rubberized materials that 'breath', others of heavy-duty canvas-like material, others of neoprene. Shop around before buying, read magazine reviews, and talk to users of each type.

Feet Cold-weather boots must be durable, insulated, and have non-skid soles.

Hands The problem with gloves tends to be that if they're thick enough to keep your hands warm they make gripping the boom difficult. The harness helps by taking some of your weight, but before donning gloves try the following acclimatization program. Go out and sail till your hands are cold but not numb. Then return to shore and slap them to restore circulation. After this you can often sail for hours, particularly if you avoid sailing on any one tack for too long since it's the front hand which usually gets coldest.

If it's too cold for this try the rubberized household gloves sold in supermarkets. Brilliant yellow is my favorite shade. You may prefer pink or blue. Some sailors cut the finger ends off for improved grip. For still colder weather wear woolen gloves inside rubberized gloves. (Wool insulates when wet.) Otherwise it may be worth buying a pair of the various special (usually expensive) boardsailing gloves.

Head Much heat is lost from the head. You'll often find that your entire body including hands remains warmer once you cover your head. A knitted woolen cap or toque serves the purpose down to around freezing point.

O'Neill's drysuit is made of neoprene. Unlike drysuits made of canvas-like and plastic materials it conforms to the body and still provides warmth should water get in

This harness has a spreader bar and removable flotation pad centered over chest and stomach to suspend the body in water-start position. Photo courtesy of Gaastra Sails USA

HARNESSES Once regarded as a luxury, harnesses are now in general use. Developed by the Charculla brothers of Germany and independently by sailors in Hawaii, acceptance occurred gradually between 1975 and 1980.

A typical harness consists of a padded vest with a hook in front for lines that you attach to either side of the boom. Qualities to look for in buying a harness include a snug fit that won't ride up, light weight, and an arrangement of webbing and back support that allows you to easily sail with your hips tilted back (in the pelvic tilt) rather than forward. Sailing with an arched back can cause lower-back problems.

A spreader bar around the hook is well worth the extra cost. This directs the pull straight out from your sides, reducing compression of the rib cage.

One type of harness that won't compress your ribs or arch your back is the hip harness, originally developed by Barry Spanier and Geoffrey Bourne of Maui Sails. Fitting over the buttocks and hips, this harness directs the strain to the sturdy hip bone and gives better balance and rig control than chest harnesses. A hip harness tends to unweight your feet in gusts however, making it most suitable with foot-strap boards.

Hip harness. Photo courtesy of Gaastra Sails USA

Harness lines Stiff, fairly heavy line hangs and hooks in best, and doesn't twist around the boom just when you need it hanging down. The line mustn't be so thick that it doesn't easily hook in and out.

Attach the lines to the boom with straps. I find that simple straps made of short pieces of webbing looped and sewn at each end stay in place better than the many more complex types.

Position the straps 80 to 90 cms apart. Adjust the length of line between them so it takes your weight while allowing you to sail with front arm more or less straight, back arm slightly bent, hands shoulder width apart. Remember that in gusts the center of effort moves back. This means the back strap mustn't be too far forward or you'll experience excessive strain on your back hand in the puffs.

Learning harness use When you can tack and gybe in 12-knot winds you're ready for a harness. Select a day with steady 8 to 12 knot wind and find calm water. Adjust line length and practice hooking in and out while on the beach. Hook in by swinging the line and catching it in the hook. Hook out by pulling the boom towards you and letting the line drop (hook down) or by bending your knees (hook up). When you practice on water, sail on a close reach.

Don't use the harness so often that you become dependent upon it. Sail without it often enough to build the endurance you'll need in tough conditions.

For racing you'll be more responsive to variations in wind when not hooked in.

STARTING UP Your ability and confidence have improved sufficiently that you feel ready to tackle higher wind. So one day when the wind picks up and raises white-caps on the water, you rig your board and go out . . . only to discover you seem to be back to square one.

Each time you lift the sail you take a ducking. Either you're catapulted off forwards or every time you sheet in the board stubbornly turns to face the wind and you fall off backwards. In fact, the techniques required for stronger wind aren't hard to master.

The stronger wind start differs from the light wind start in that before sheeting in you tilt the mast across the board to windward, and you actually lean back slightly ahead of sheeting in.

However, first you must pull the sail up without slipping a disc. Keeping knees bent and back straight, lean back and use body weight and thigh muscles to haul the sail up. When the wind is pressing it down particularly strongly, pulling the mast slightly towards the wind and wiggling the board back and forth with your feet helps break the sail free. Once water has drained from the sail, pull it up steadily, without delay. The sooner it's clear of the water the better, because it becomes easier to hold.

Holding the sail completely clear of the water, point the board on a close reach, the easiest course to get started on. Grasp the boom with your front hand, then tilt the mast forward and well to windward, the sail still luffing.

Space your feet fairly far apart. The front foot mustn't be too far forward or the board's nose may be driven under-water like a sounding whale as it starts moving. Front foot alongside the mast works well.

Grip the boom with your back hand. Now, as you sheet in, lean back towards the water. If you sheet in too much you'll be pulled forward into the water. If you don't sheet in enough you'll fall back into the water.

Don't bend forward at the waist. Try to fill the sail a little while keeping it tilted forward and to windward, and drive the board forward with a straight front leg. If you are pulled forward on sheeting in, luff the sail immediately and take your weight on your legs again. Make sure you're headed on a close reach, then fall back and sheet in again. Drop your body back in gradual stages to fill the sail bit by bit until you're able to fill it completely and go full speed. When you're in better control of the sail and are using it to main-tain balance, move your feet closer together.

HINTS TO KEEP IN MIND

1 Initially you may find that to stop your board stubbornly turning its nose into the wind in those critical seconds after sheeting in, you have to push the nose off the wind with the front foot and pull the tail around with your back foot. You'll use this less as you improve.

2 When you first try to get going in stronger wind you may not lean out enough, so imagine you're playing tug-of-war with the boom.

3 At this point you may discover that your feet start slip-ping. You can improve your traction by waxing the board or

Figure 1 *Dorothy Berry drives the board forward with her front foot turned slightly forward, hanging her weight on the boom with front arm extended and back arm bent*

Figure 2 *Beach practice. For a broad reach the body moves back on the board, allowing the front to plane out of the water. Unless your board has a mast track the sail must be raked back*

wearing boardsailing shoes. However it may also be a matter of technique. Try hanging more weight on the boom, transfering driving force from your feet to the mast.

4 If a sudden lull drops you back, crouch immediately to avoid falling. If necessary grab the mast low down with your front hand to crouch lower, increasing the sail's leverage over your body.

STANCE Don't worry about stance at first but as you gain confidence aim for the technique shown in figures 1 and 2.

As the wind increases and you lean back to counter it, try to hang your weight on the boom as if your arms are cables and your hands hooks, rather than pulling back with every muscle tensed.

Don't space your feet farther apart than necessary. Turn the front foot towards the front and move it nearer the windward rail. The back leg is slightly more bent than the front and supports more weight. Feet and hands move farther apart and farther back as the wind increases. The mast should be upright or inclined towards the wind somewhat.

For sensitive and relaxed control, extend the front arm and bend the rear arm slightly, hands positioned so each feels equal pull. This arrangement allows you to rake the mast forward or back with the front hand while sensitively adjusting sheeting angle with the back hand.

CHOPPY WATER Choppy water demands you set sail quickly and tack smoothly. Don't stand struggling for the perfect start-up position before sheeting in. As long as your sail is luffing you're vulnerable to even the smallest of waves. But with the stabilizing influence of a full sail in your hands, balance becomes much easier.

When tacking concentrate on getting to the other side of the sail rapidly, so that if you start to fall backward all you have to do is pull in with your back hand.

GUSTS Watch the water ahead for gusts, which you'll see as darker patches of ripples moving with the wind, and prepare to react quickly to the increased force.

Gusts tend to bring shifts in wind direction. In offshore winds these shifts are often major and the safest way to weather them is to balance yourself unaided by the sail and sheet out a moment before the gust hits. When the gust eases and you've identified the new direction, sheet in again.

In less shifty wind, when a good gust tries to pull you over and makes the board head up, luff the sail a little and tilt it forward slightly. If you don't rake the sail forward when you unsheet you'll head up. If on the other hand you don't luff but try to lean out and sheet in harder, you're likely to be unsuccessful and head up anyway, or cause the board to rail up, or be catapulted.

BEARING OFF Bearing off from a close reach or close-hauled course becomes harder as the wind increases. You need to lean the sail forward, yet you need to move your weight back to counter the sail. Since telescopic arms aren't readily available, try this technique: a) Adopt a wide stance, placing the front foot forward near the windward rail and the back foot behind the centerboard well near the lee rail; b) Crouch; c) Move your hands further apart and slightly further back and lean the mast forward and to windward; d) Sheet in for extra power and push the nose downwind with your front foot while pulling the tail around towards the wind with your back foot. As the board turns, sheet out steadily.

The board bears off more readily if you push the windward rail down with the front foot. Keep the ball of the back foot near the lee rail to stop it rising too far.

Once you're on a beam reach you can move your body further back on the board if you want to turn faster.

It's possible you'll be catapulted the first few times you try bearing off in heavy air. The sail will suddenly pull very strongly. You'll pull back, but the sail will prove stronger and you'll find yourself in the water in front of the board. To avoid this, keep the sail near its luffing point by sheeting in and out steadily and rapidly to avoid committing yourself to a setting you can't handle.

RAILING When reaching in wind over about 12 knots with the centerboard fully down, you'll find the sailboard becomes very unstable, rolling from side to side and even tipping over. This is called *railing*.

The solution is to retract the centerboard if your equipment allows this, otherwise to sweep it back or pull it partway up. If sweeping it back or pulling it up partway doesn't cure the problem, pull it out entirely and hang it on your arm.

To withdraw a centerboard, luff on a beach reach. Keep the mast forward and to weather to maintain heading, then reach down quickly with your back hand. With the centerboard removed it can be difficult to get going again because you tend to slip sideways or head up. Tilt the luffing sail forward to turn the board below a beam reach. Lean back, sheet in, and drive the board off the wind with your front foot.

The windward edge of the board can even rail up when sailing upwind, usually because your sail is too large, your centerboard is too large, or the sail is leaned too far to windward, leaving too little of your weight on the windward rail. If sailing with the rig as near vertical as possible and your feet on the windward rail doesn't stop the railing, rake the centerboard back a few degrees or lift it vertically in its slot slightly. Lifting the centerboard vertically best preserves its efficiency.

HEAVY AIR (Force 5 and over)

Upwind Since in heavy air a significant proportion of the sail may be luffing, depending in part upon the rig's efficiency, its center of effort is generally further back. Therefore your hands also move back, positioned so each experiences equal pull.

Both feet are placed near the windward rail to prevent it railing up, the back foot taking more weight than the front. Footstraps make sailing easier, helping keep you on the board and giving more control over rig and board.

Fatigue is one of the problems to confront you, usually waiting till you're some distance from shore before making its appearance. Fight fatigue by being relaxed. A boardsailing harness is your best high-wind safety device.

Off the wind You'll have to fully retract or withdraw the centerboard when sailing on courses below a beam reach.

While at slower speeds you want to be forward on the board for maximum speed, at planing speeds you move back, allowing the front to rise out of the water and thus reducing drag.

And whereas at slow speeds you can turn upwind slightly by dipping the lee rail, at planing speeds you can turn upwind slightly by dipping the windward rail and turn downwind by dipping the lee rail. This is known as carving a turn.

Bearing off. Notice how Marina pushes the tail of the board towards the wind with the ball of her back foot while her front foot pushes the nose downwind

Push the windward rail down with your front foot to bear off faster

1

2

5

6

3

4

7

FLARE GYBE For a high-wind flare gybe follow the technique for gybing in moderate wind but keep the mast leaned back so you aren't pulled forward, and stand further back to exert greater turning force on the board. You'll need to position your feet near each rail and keep your weight over your hips so you can push down on either rail as the need arises. In the photosequence Mark Robinson of Clearwater Beach, Florida shows how it's done.

Here in summary is a typical flare gybe.

While sailing on a beam reach, luff momentarily so you can step or jump back on the board and move your hands slightly nearer the clew and further apart. For a tight turn jump back far enough to sink the tail. To maintain high boat speed stay further forward so the board remains flatter.

With hands and feet in position, rig raked back and well to windward, sheet in strongly. As the nose turns downwind, push the tail around the other way with your feet. If you dip the windward rail to start the board turning, be sure to level the board off or bank it the other way before you reach the new tack or else an oncoming wave may catch it, lift it and throw you off balance. Let the sail flip around and sheet in on the new tack as soon as you can.

You can have tremendous fun with this gybe, turning sharply on the tail fin or in a broad spray-throwing arc like a waterskier.

Railing Leaving the centerboard down gives a sharper, less mushy flare gybe than pulling it up. However with the centerboard down in waves and swells you'll discover that unless you do something to prevent waves dramatically accelerating the board as it bears off, it'll rail up and you'll be thrown off. To avoid picking up so much speed try one or another of these three methods: a) Bear off more sharply by using your back foot to pull the tail around, giving the board less time to gather speed; b) Time your bearing off to avoid being picked up by a wave. Instead, bear off onto the back of a wave so it slows the board; c) Luff just below a broad reach, jump back, and sink the tail sufficiently to stall the board's forward motion. If the board spins back onto the original tack when you sink the tail, you're probably sinking the lee rail by mistake. Remember that pressing the left rail down makes the board turn right, and vice versa. Good control of waist and leg muscles is essential. It's also essential to step forward again quickly as you reach the new tack, otherwise the board will continue turning into the wind.

Option two, slowing the board against the back of a wave, is safest.

POWER GYBE Before passing on to other topics it's worth mentioning the power gybe and its relative the push gybe.

For a power gybe you release the boom and step one foot in front of the mast, holding the mast with the back hand. Pause to steady yourself and slow down, then grab the other side of the boom with your front hand and sheet in on the other side of the sail. Pull the nose downwind and around onto the new tack while pushing the board around with your feet.

This makes for a very tight turn in circumstances where you can't gybe any other way. I've seen Matt Schweitzer win the slalom at a Windsurfer World Championships using this gybe against the world's best while they used flare gybes.

Push gybe Bear off as for running and flare gybes, but before you're dead downwind, back the sail (fill it from the back) by pushing on the boom. Push gently to push the board through the eye of the wind.

Power gybe

Freestyle – performing unusual maneuvers in a graceful fashion. It can be just for fun or for competition. Either way it greatly improves your all-round board-handling skills.

Today's freestyle contests are a blend of gymnastics, dance, self-expression and sailing which evolved during the mid-1970s from hotdogging displays by inventive young Americans. In the first edition of *The Wind is Free*, Ken Winner and I – both freestyle enthusiasts – put together a satire on the attitudes of the stereotyped hotdogger. We directed the piece as much at ourselves as at others, though it wasn't always read that way. One of the many responses it provoked was a counter-satire in the British magazine *ON BOARD*, entitled "The Wind can be Expensive" by a fictitious Fred Loser. With the magazine's permission their article is reprinted here, following the original.

The Wind is Free
by Roger Jones and Ken Winner

"Late Saturday morning you come cruisin' out to the beach, your sailboard atop your cool green MG. You check out the scene: the sun hot enough to melt the sand, the sand covered with beach towels, beach towels covered with girls, and the girls hot enough to boil the sea. You gaze through your shades at the sun, the girls, the white-capping water, and say to yourself "Awwright", cause you're cool, you're the Freestyle Kid.

Casually, but carefully, you rig the board, conscious of curious glances straying your way. Now is no time to trip over your mast.

You push the board to the water. Adrenalin starts to pump and your mind clicks into gear with the 15-knot breeze. It's just you and your board on a date with wind and water."

After describing the impressive moves performed, our narrator continues: "You land the board, the amateur photographers scatter, and you flop down in the sand to soak up its heat. Rolling onto your back into warmer sand, sighing with satisfaction, you lay an arm across your eyes to shade out the sun. Then a voice disturbs your reverie. "Excuse me, is this a sail surfer?" In the glare of the sun stands someone brown, with long blond hair and a white bikini. You smile, but not too broadly ('cause you're cool), and say to yourself, "Aww-right!"

The Wind can be Expensive
by Fred Loser

Very late Sunday afternoon you bump-start your old VW and drive down to the beach. It's miserably cold and raining, and your hangover hasn't quite disappeared. Your cold, wet, wet-suit smells slightly in your slightly-moulding carrier bag. You change in the drizzle and drag your board over the sharp shingle to the murky water.

Rigging your craft you curse yourself for not replacing your inhaul line – it snaps for the umpteenth time, so you have to use your other shoe-lace. You still can't find two of your battens – but what the hell – you're here to enjoy yourself – you're the British Windsurfing Kid.

You cart your tatty equipment to the water's edge, aware of a small crowd of people laughing behind their hands. Now is the time you trip over the mast. You put the board

in the water and go back to fetch the rig. When you get that to the water you go back to fetch the board – which has been flung ashore by disrespectful waves. Then you fetch the sail again . . . then the board . . . and so on. Finally, board, sail and you are in the right place – and you're ready to go. You study the sea assiduously and stare at the oncoming breakers – sometimes every wave just seems to mock you. You launch – and that's the moment the amateur photographer bursts into action (see photo).

Your trick produces an insurance claim for a broken dagger-plate and a ripped sail.

You paddle back to shore and stuff your equipment in the boot of your car where the sail can pick up rust and oil stains, and lug your board onto the roof-rack.

Having changed back into clothes (no underpants 'cos you wore them under your wet-suit) you climb back into the driving seat but are interrupted by an inquisitive senior citizen who says: "You must be mad to do that in this weather".

You smile, but not too much ('cos you're knackered) and say: "Yeah, you're right".

Fred Loser: "Just you and your board on a date with wind and water"

LEARNING A TRICK Learning is quicker and more enjoyable if you first think each stage of the trick through, clearly visualizing each movement. Identify the difficult aspects and, having understood the forces involved, devise ways to minimize the difficulty. Study photos. Watch experts and novices to gain a thorough understanding of what to do and what not to do. Discuss the moves with friends and add their insights to your considerations.

Begin practice in the livingroom with an imaginary board (you only need to worry when it starts talking back to you), then move to the beach for some land practice with the actual equipment. When you try the move on water, choose conditions as near ideal as you can find.

COMPETITIONS For competitive freestyle you'll need a routine composed of tricks that flow one into the next and keep you moving, always positioned where the judges can clearly see what you're doing.

Study the points-awarding system so you're clear about what you must do to score well. Adapt your moves according to conditions during the event, and don't try for moves so difficult you aren't sure of succeeding.

Originality is as important as a snappy, refined performance. Often the competitor who surprises the judges carries off first prize. Keep an eye on what other competitors are doing so you don't do the same or similar moves. An appropriately novel final move or dismount is particularly important.

SELECTED TRICKS Hundreds of tricks exist and new moves are constantly being developed. To give some idea of what's possible, a few moves are illustrated here. If you want to know more about freestyle, my book *Freestyle Windsurfing with Gary Eversole* goes into much more detail.

Sitdown Tricks don't all have to be strenuous. Elegance can be sufficient. Kelby Anno of Maui, Hawaii, uses this sitdown as the lead-in to a light-air head dip.

Splits Before trying splits on a board, be able to do the splits on land. Before actually performing the move, warm up with some stretching exercises.

Facing Back of Sail American freestyle champion Lisa Penfield Edwards demonstrates how a very simple move can be made more interesting. Adding one move to another like this is the essence of freestyle.

Inside the Boom Here Lisa sails inside the boom facing the wind. This is easiest on a close reach. One way into position is by first crossing your hands on the boom, selecting an underhand grip for the hand you move in front. You can then duck inside the boom and turn around without releasing the boom as you go.

Head Dip Head dips are easiest in steady, moderate wind. The basic head dip is performed while sailing normally and is fairly easy to learn, very easy to do once you've learned the knack. Simply arch your back, lean well back, sheet out enough to drop yourself back until you can dip your head, then sheet in to pull yourself up again. I usually bear off to just below a close reach for extra power as I lean back. It's also fun to sail along looking at the water upside-down for a while.

The back-to-sail head dip which Lisa performs here is slightly harder. First you must turn your back to the sail and stabilize yourself in that position. To turn, luff and transfer the back hand to the mast, then turn your back to the sail while simultaneously releasing the front hand and placing it some way back on the boom. In moderate wind you can lean forward and do a head dip (or nose dip) from this position. In light wind move your back hand down to the foot of the sail and your front hand down the mast, so the rig exerts more leverage over you.

Back-to-Back There are a number of ways to position yourself with your back to the leeside of the sail. You can simply stop sailing, luff, step around to the front of the sail, and sheet in by leaning back. Alternatively you could sail clew-first, let the clew flip over the bow and, as the sail swings around, step quickly in front of the mast, throwing the sail behind your back and sheeting in. This latter sequence isn't difficult if performed quickly and vigorously. The back-to-back is illustrated by Marina Lari, a boardsailing enthusiast and fashion designer.

Ducktack This doesn't mean to tack like a duck but to duck under the sail as you tack. Bring the board head-to-wind or very slightly past head-to-wind, release your back hand and throw the luffing sail directly into the eye of the wind, sliding your front hand back along the boom. Then quickly step to the other side of the board, pulling the sail back down as you go. Speedy execution makes this easier, so you reach the new side of the sail ready to sheet in before the sail can refill on either side.

Railride Canadian boardsailor and writer Steve Jarrett performs a forward railride, probably the most popular of all tricks. Always tighten the mastfoot before railriding so it doesn't pop out unexpectedly, and reinforce the end of your mast if you plan to railride often.

1 Lift the windward rail by pulling it up with the side of your forward foot while pushing the lee rail down with the other foot. When your balance improves you may wish to try lifting the windward rail by hooking the arch of your foot or the underside of your heel over it, so you can stand on the rail immediately it pops up without the painful intermediate "shin on the rail" stage. The rail pops up fairly easily if you transfer your weight suddenly to the boom when the board is tilted at about 45°.

2 As the board reaches vertical, take all your weight on the boom, transfer the back foot to the windward rail, and slip the other down onto the centerboard beside the hull. The more of your weight you take on the boom the less you'll bruise your shin. Using an underhand grip for your forward hand makes it easier to take your weight on the boom.

3 Balance is relatively easy with one foot on the centerboard counterbalancing the other foot on the rail, but don't put weight on the centerboard at any distance from the hull, or you'll crack the centerboard. Avoid pressing the rail heavily against the mast. You'll split the mast – if the mastfoot doesn't pop out first.

4 Balance becomes more critical once both feet are on the rail. You must rely on weight shifts and on sheeting in and out to correct the slightest tilting. Keep glancing down at the rail. If it tilts to leeward, sheet out because the sail is pulling you over. If the rail tilts to windward sheet in to pull it back up immediately.

If you start the railride when on a course closer than 90° to the wind the board will steadily turn into the wind and you'll soon have to back the sail to stay up. However if you start at 90° to the wind, or a few degrees further off the wind to allow for some heading up as you raise the rail, the board will stay on a steady course.

After the effort it took at first to get the rail up and stay on it, you may be surprised to discover that once the board is well balanced, it doesn't want to come down and you may have to sheet out and determinedly lever the rail down.

Back-to-Sail Stern-First Railride This sequence conveys the panache that helped Andrea Livingston become a Windsurfer World Champion. Raising the board onto its rail is easier when sailing stern-first than when sailing forward, because the fin tends to grab and help flip the board up. Here Andrea has raised the daggerboard slightly and levers down on the top of it to lift the rail.

7

TRIANGLE RACING

Racing can be many things – a few hours with friends, serious competition, or the way you earn your sponsorship money. If you're new to racing this chapter will get you started. Funboard racing is introduced in the high-performance section of the book, though many topics apply in both forms of racing.

RULES

Read the rules, or at very least a summary of the important rules. Many triangle races are run under International Yacht Racing Union (IYRU) rules which are in a booklet available from most national sailing authorities.

THE COURSE

One-design class regattas and races run under IYRU rules often use the Olympic course in figure 1, or a variation of it which uses the same line for both start and finish, placing this line between marks 1 and 3. This course puts emphasis on upwind sailing, whereas funboard races emphasize reaching and gybing.

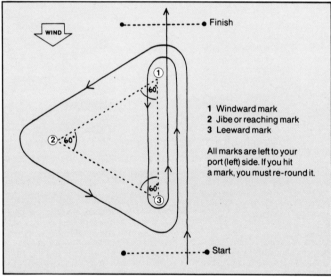

1 Windward mark
2 Jibe or reaching mark
3 Leeward mark

All marks are left to your port (left) side. If you hit a mark, you must re-round it.

Figure 1 Olympic course

SKIPPERS' MEETING

Most races are preceded by skippers' meetings. Attend them – not so you can enjoy the sight of weatherbeaten ancient mariners wearing fisherman's knit and sucking on pipes, but so you can review sailing instructions, answer queries and deal with amendments. Important things you'll learn include the course markers, starting time, and the sequence of flag raisings or sounds which will indicate how much time is left before the start.

STARTING

The start is one of the most important parts of the race, particularly a short race. If you get behind at the start you have to try to catch up with the leaders while suffering the disadvantage of disturbed air left by the passage of many other sails.

The line

The start is a line of sight between two starting marks or boats, or a boat and a mark. If you're over the line before the signal, even just a few centimeters over, race committee spotters will call your number and you'll have to restart or be disqualified.

Starting sequence

Before the starting signal comes a sequence of flag raisings, horn honkings etc., telling how much time is left before the start. A waterproof watch that counts down is a great help in keeping track of time.

Favored end

In practice one end of the line is often a significant distance upwind of the other. This is the favored end.

Five or ten minutes before the start, find the favored end by the procedure shown in figure 2. Luff near one end and aim your board at the other. Whichever end the front of your boom points most nearly towards is the favored end. If neither end is favored the sail will be perpendicular to the board's centerline.

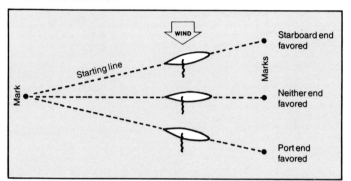

Starboard end favored

Neither end favored

Port end favored

Figure 2 Determine the favored end of the line

Starting at the upwind end puts you ahead of those who don't start there. Unfortunately most people can work this out, so there's usually a milling, barging crowd at the favored end. Until you have excellent board-handling and starting abilities, stay clear of the crowd and start about a third of the way down the line. Though this may not give you the best start it won't give you the worst.

Bargers

Figure 3 illustrates bargers trying to squeeze in at the favored end. The boards within circle A all try to squeeze between board B and the official start boat C. Board B isn't obliged to let any boards in and anyone pushing in regardless is barging. This is illegal. It's also self-defeating because all those bargers, of whom only a couple will get a good start, leave the rest of the line less cluttered for circumspect sailors like D.

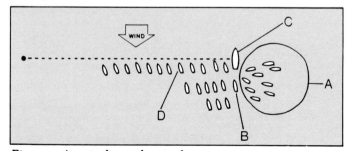

Figure 3 A typical start showing barging

Final 30 seconds

As the starting sequence counts down people jockey for position. At 30 seconds to go make sure you're in or near the first row of boards. Those near you help indicate where the line is. Just keep the front of your board even with the front of boards either side, then with two or three seconds left, sheet in and go.

BEATING Having started, your next objective is to reach the windward mark in minimum time. Seek clean air and point as high as you can without slipping sideways. When you feel the board slipping sideways, bear off to gain speed.

Windshifts Every few minutes the wind changes direction by a few degrees. These shifts affect the distance you must sail to reach the windward mark. Shifts which make you point lower to maintain speed (*headers*) cause you to sail a greater distance – unless you tack. Hence the maxim *Tack when headed*. Conversely, a windshift which allows you to point nearer the mark and still maintain speed (a *lift*), reduces the distance you must sail. More on windshifts later.

REACHING AND RUNNING As wind and waves pick up you may have difficulty staying on your feet when reaching and running. Pulling the centerboard out or retracting it helps if the problem is centerboard plane. For reaching in lighter wind the centerboard can give extra stability and reduce sideslip.

Steer so as to surf swells and chop. Stand far enough back to stop the bow digging into waves.

If someone is close behind as you start a reaching leg, point high so he or she doesn't block your wind then triumphantly pass by. And when running, especially in light air, get off to the side of the group of sails behind.

FINISHING Finish lines often aren't square to the wind and therefore have a favored end, the downwind end. Avoid sailing further than necessary. In particular, avoid sailing parallel to the line. Try to cross it on whichever tack is most nearly perpendicular, with the mark positioned just to leeward of you (figure 4).

When neither end of the line is particularly favored try to make your final approach on starboard tack, so you've right of way in any last minute encounters.

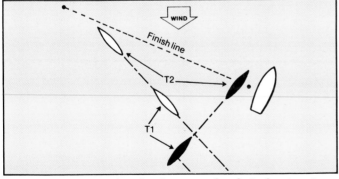

Figure 4 At time T1 *the white boat was ahead. At this time the black boat tacked, and at time T2 crossed the favored end of the line to win*

Kai Schnellbacher
HiFly World Cup Team

ADVANCED HINTS

Tactics and strategy The necessity for tactics and strategy makes racing an intellectual activity and you'll do well to study some books on the subjects.

Tactics involve maneuvering to gain advantage over opponents through position and use of rules. Strategy involves a game plan for the entire race and considerations such as whether to take the left or right side of the course for the beat, whether to plan for currents or tidal flow etc.

Windshifts If the wind shifts only very slightly or if it's oscillating back and forth rapidly, don't tack on being headed. You'll lose too much ground by repeatedly coming about. Tack only when reasonably sure you'll gain upwind advantage.

Saying this is easy. The tough bit comes in recognizing that you've been headed. Here are six indicators.

1 *The balance point of the boom shifts back.* What you feel is an increase in pressure on the back hand as a header luffs the front part of the sail. Boardsailors who don't race tend to miss shifts because they develop the habit of unconsciously adjusting the sail's angle of attack to keep the pull on each hand equal.

2 *Feel and hear the board slow, stall, increase sideslip.* Learn to sense changes through your feet. When sideslip increases, the hull's movements feel different. The sound of the water also changes. Similarly with decreased forward speed.

3 *Feel the wind change direction on your cheeks* – The cheeks of your face that is, unless you're at a Club Med.

4 *Observe windshifts change the pattern on the water surface ahead.*

5 *Nearby boards change their angle relative to you.* If boards ahead suddenly point lower, they've been headed, so be ready to react to a header. If boards close behind suddenly point higher than you, chances are you just failed to detect a header. When observing other boards it's important not to become obsessed with other skippers' technique, how much they're tilting the hull, foot position etc. This can destroy your concentration and make you lose the race.

6 *Notice your angle change relative to markers, reference points ashore, etc.* Each time you tack, note your heading relative to some distinctive stationary object and keep an eye on it.

Regard the last two methods of spotting shifts as secondary to the first four. Sensitivity to wind, water, rig and board are the keys to success. The closer together your hands the more easily you notice changes in wind strength and direction. The same goes for your feet. In addition to feeling changes through your hands and arms, learn to feel them throughout your body. Many top competitors consider that sailing with back bowed out slightly, enables them to feel variations in the boom's pull through the sensitive areas either side of the lower spine.

Balance point of the boom For simplicity, assume that the sail transmits Force **F** by the mast, and Force **R** by the clew. *Figure 1* shows the situation with the sail properly trimmed. When the wind shifts to head you, the magnitude

of **F** is reduced while **R** remains approximately constant (*Figure 2*). Hence the pull on the back hand increases – the same sensation occurs when a gust bends the mast and luffs the fore part of the sail.

Stalling the rig (a lift) has the opposite effect, though to a lesser extent. The balance point moves forward, causing the force taken by the forward hand to increase (*Figure 3*).

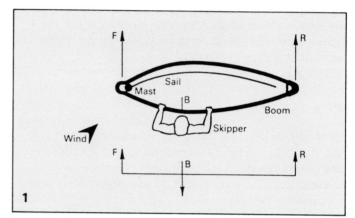

Figure 1 Sail correctly trimmed: Imagine the boom as a balance with the sailor as the fulcrum at B1 which is the balance point of the boom. (The sailor's hands are equidistant either side of the balance point.) In this situation the turning moment created by F is exactly counterbalanced by the turning moment created by R

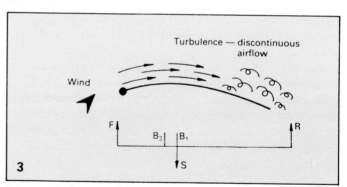

Figure 2 A header luffs the sail: When a heading windshift occurs, the fore part of the sail luffs (see it flutter and flap) reducing the force on F. R remains constant, and so the force on the back hand increases. The new balance point of the sail becomes B2

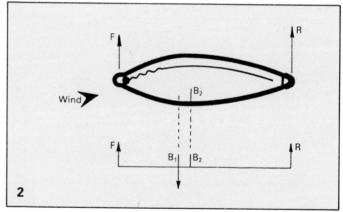

Figure 3 Lifting windshift stalls the sail: Force on R is reduced while F remains constant. Therefore pressure on the forward hand increases and the new balance point becomes B3 which is forward of B1

Equipment Ensure that your sail, hull and centerboard are in best possible condition. A racing sail shouldn't have been used so much it's stretched or deformed. When rigged it must be free of creases and major wrinkles. Sand down or fill in scratches on the hull. Use a centerboard with an efficient foil shape, its size correctly matched with sail size and fin size.

Hull trim To sail upwind, tilt the leeward rail down a few degrees to increase lateral resistance, enabling you to sail a higher course. Displacement hulls should be tilted more than flatboards.

In chop and swells move back and forth as necessary to keep the bow from burying and to help initiate planing or surfing.

Pumping Under IYRU rules three successive pumps of the sail are allowed for the purpose of accelerating down a wave (surfing) and to initiate planing in response to increased wind. Apart from this, steady, rhythmic, noticeable pumping is likely to result in a protest.

To pump upwind or when reaching, lean the sail to leeward then pull it towards your body, thrusting the board forward.

Downwind it's more effective to paddle from side to side as if you're in a kayak. Instead of simply pulling the sail straight towards your body, pull it slightly to left or right and towards your body.

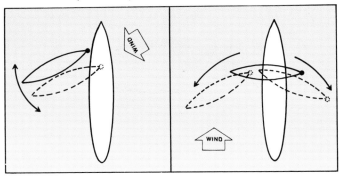

Upwind As you sail upwind you often see rough and smooth patches of water. Point high in smooth patches and bear off in rough patches for extra speed to pound through.

When you're planing in a particularly smooth patch it sometimes pays to bear off a bit for more speed, then head up an extra bit so you don't sail below the mark, then bear off again before your speed dissipates, and so on. As you head up, maintain speed by sheeting in and pushing with the back foot.

Oncoming waves tend to check your speed, so pull on the sail and thrust with your back leg to power through. To get over a steep wave head up slightly so it doesn't push you sideways, then bear away down the back to regain speed.

This is always supposing there's enough wind for these steering actions. In light air there's nothing for it but to point high and slog on.

Reaching On a reaching leg a higher angle of sail is generally faster than a lower angle. A good rule of thumb is to head up slightly in the lulls to maintain boat speed and bear off in the puffs to stay on course.

However there are times in light wind and large chop when a lower point of sail is faster because it allows you to surf continuously down across waves.

Surfing greatly increases your speed. To catch a wave give your first pump just before it reaches you, and the second pump when you're in the trough in front of it. This may be all it takes. If not, give your last legal pump when the board is almost lifted to the top of the wave, and try to accelerate down its face. With enough speed you can overtake the wave in front and surf down its face.

If the wave you're on is about to leave you behind, head up a bit to maintain speed, preparing to catch the wave behind. Otherwise you'll be left wallowing, with no speed to catch it.

Mark rounding In a crowd, a push or power gybe gives a tight, controlled turn at the reaching mark. A sharp flare gybe is fastest if there's room.

Be careful not to stall the centerboard or the sail at the leeward mark. Turn smoothly, not sharply.

Attitude Attitude is critical to success. You must have a fierce desire to win, the belief that you can win, and the mental discipline to do what's necessary to win. Rare is the person who wins consistently without such an attitude.

SECTION TWO
Funboards & High Performance

Craig Yester at Backyards
on Oahu's north shore

High-performance means high-speed maneuvering on a board with footstraps, high aspect ratio sail and short boom. The techniques require wind of 12 to 15 knots or more and apply to sinkers, semi-sinkers and transitional boards. A sinker is a board which sinks under the rider's weight when not planing. A semi-sinker can just about be uphauled if conditions aren't too rough. The term isn't absolute, of course. A heavy person's sinker may be a light person's floater. Transitional boards are of mid-length and have full uphaul capacity.

Making the transition from traditional long board sailing to high-performance isn't difficult, though it requires some relearning. Handling high wind and waves is easier using modern high-performance equipment than using an old-fashioned long board, pinhead sail and full-length boom.

CONTRIBUTORS This section was written on the Hawaiian island of Maui based on discussions with Maui Meyer, Fred Haywood (who also acted as technical editor), Alex Aguera, Doug Hunt, Vince D'Onofrio, Rob Kniskern, Barry Spanier and Geoffrey Bourne (Maui Sails), Monty Spindler (Neil Pryde Sails), Marty Langford (Gaastra Sails), and board shaper Jimmy Lewis. Patrick Hough of Freesport in Ontario, Canada gave advice regarding boards for lakes and small surf. Darrell Wong took the wave riding and jumping photos except where otherwise stated. Roger Jones took the carve, duck and snap gybes, chop jumps, waterstarts, launching, landing etc.

Maui Meyer

Fred Haywood

Barry Spanier

Darrell Wong

EQUIPMENT 8

Asymmetric board made for Hookipa

BOARDS Suit your board to your ability and to the conditions where you sail. For example, in the mushy waves of Europe and on lakes you need a wider flatter thicker-railed board than for well-formed regular Hawaiian-style waves. This shape doesn't carve as well as a thin-railed narrow Hawaiian board, but you can pivot it quickly and it accelerates rapidly.

Before buying a production hull, test-sail it. Until you're an expert yourself, commission a custom hull only from a shaper who understands the conditions where you'll sail. Take his advice on shape and dimensions and test-sail similar boards before parting with your money.

Bearing in mind that boards are very sensitive to the weight of the rider, here are guidelines on board dimension and sailing characteristics.

Sinker Length 2.1-2.6m. Widest point 51-58.½ cm. Once water-starting and gybing are mastered sinkers are exciting and relatively easy to sail given 18 knots of wind or more.

Semi-sinker Length 2.5-2.9 m. Widest point up to 61cm. These boards need at least 10 knots of wind, the water whitecapping, before the fun begins.

Transitional (full uphaul capability) Length 2.9-3.2m. Widest point 58-61cm. When you've mastered tacking and gybing in 12-knot winds you're ready for a transitional board. Some have sliding mast tracks and retractable centerboards. They can be jumped, surfed and carved, though not as well as shorter boards.

Race Length up to 4m. Widest point 61-63½ cm. Narrow tails. Some displacement at the front, large planing area towards the back. Large skegs. Weight 13½-15½kg. Race boards have good upwind performance, while flat and V-bottoms combined with narrow tails allow planing and carved turns.

ROCKER The upward curve of a board's underside at nose and tail is called rocker. Nose rocker (often termed scoop) helps stop the nose digging in. Tail rocker promotes turning but makes boards slower and reduces pointing ability.

Short boards for radical waves need less nose scoop and more tail rocker than longer, wider boards for choppy lake conditions and slalom-type sailing. Nose scoop for a wave board is typically 15 to 18 cm, for a lake/slalom board 18 to 25 cm. Tail rocker for a radical wave board might be 6 cm, for slalom and lake-sailing 3 to 4 cm.

TAILS The width, thickness and shape of tails affect turning and jumping characteristics. Wide tails give more thrust off waves for jumping, but because they're harder to depress than narrow tails they don't carve turns as readily. Suitable width for speed, chop jumping, small waves and tight turns is about 35 to 40 cms measured at 30cm from the tail end. For tighter turns on larger waves, use a narrower tail so you can easily sink the rail and make it bite and grip well.

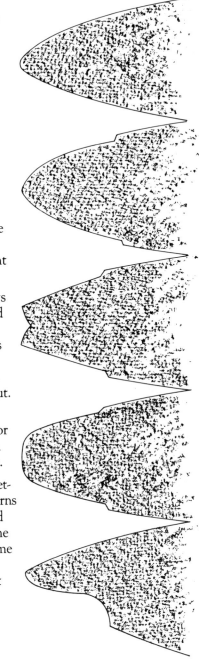

Round pintail Gives a long smooth carving turn, maintaining good speed and control, but not considered as good for carving sharp turns as winged pintails.

Winged pintail In general wings are put on tails to allow width to be stepped down without increasing overall taper. Keeping area underfoot promotes planing while decreasing area behind the wings makes the tail sink and grip better during tight turns.

Swallowtail Theory says a swallowtail gives a broad area for planing yet functions like two narrow tails during tight turns, when one side of the board is in the water and the other out.

Squashtail Good for surfing small waves and for jumping, but its large area makes it skittery on turns.

Asymmetrics Asymmetric tails improve surfing turns when consistent wind and wave direction result in the sailor always using the same rail for the same kind of turn. The long drawn-out side is used for bottom turns (see wave riding chapter) and the shorter side for tight, snappy cutbacks.

FINS A large single fin is effective on race boards and narrow wave boards. A three-fin arrangement is better on wide tails, though slower. The popular thruster arrangement has a large central fin with two identical smaller fins set slightly further forward and toed inward to lead into turns.

When air becomes trapped around the fin and stops it from gripping, it's said to ventilate or cavitate. Many designs have been developed to stop air becoming trapped on the fin, including fins with horizontal ridges or fences, boomerang shapes, fins with narrow necks and large football-shaped ends.

If you do feel your fin sliding sideways after a jump or turn, try slowing down and rocking the tail from side to side to shift the air pocket.

Shaper Patrick Hough with boards for lake sailing

MAST EXTENSIONS Because sails of different size and cut have different mast pocket lengths you'll need an adjustable extension on the bottom of your mast if you want to be equipped for a broad range of conditions. Ensure that the extension fits into the mast without sloppiness or it will develop leverage and crack the end of the mast. Pad out slackness with tape or something tough like sail fabric. Reinforcing the mast end is a good idea too.

Mast pads To protect your board from damage, wrap a mast pad around the exposed part of both mast and extension.

ADJUSTABLE BOOMS Different sails require different boom lengths, so an adjustable boom is a must. Each type has its pros and cons. An advantage of those with different length endpieces is that changing the ends as required gives them less chance to seize solid than telescopic booms. On the other hand it's dismaying to be at the beach half-rigged only to discover you left the required endpieces at home.

Stiff spars are essential. Boom ends must be tough enough to take a beating. A pulley system or rollers on the back will make outhauling easier.

FOOTSTRAPS Be sure your strap openings are the correct size. For safe surfing you must be able to slip your foot in without fumbling, and be able to withdraw it easily when you have to. If your foot goes too far into the strap you won't be able to get it out swiftly, particularly if you're falling. Adjust the strap so no more than your toes stick out the front, as illustrated. When correctly fitted, lifting your toes will lock your feet in the strap.

It's generally accepted that Larry ('Stan') Stanley of Windsurfing Hawaii in Kailua was the first person to fit straps to a board – though it's possible that, as with many of mankind's inventions, someone else somewhere else fitted straps earlier. In late 1976 or early 1977, as far as those involved recall the dates, Stan fitted straps to a 3.2-meter, 16-kilogram double-tunnel custom hull that he called the Rocket Chip. His original intention was to make it manageable at high speed. In this he was partially successful, but the Chip pearled easily and so, although Stan realised that straps gave control on waves, he put the board away and concentrated on learning new moves on his Windsurfer. The concept of footstraps lay dormant until early 1978, when Jürgen Hönscheid of West Germany visited Hawaii and rekindled Stan's enthusiasm for wave jumping. At this time they were jumping without straps, mostly jumping and bailing out. Then Stan recalled the Chip, dug it out of storage, and started jumping with footstraps. Others soon fitted straps to their boards and, to quote Stan, "That's when we started discovering controlled flight."

Strap placement If positioning your own straps, first sail the board to identify where you place your feet. Take a pencil out with you (because a pencil makes marks when wet) and when you find a good foot position, mark the deck. Bear in mind that you tend to stand further forward without straps because an upright posture feels safer. In particular, measure the separation of both feet in your most comfortable stance.

Rear straps Typically, the rearmost strap insert is placed no further back than the trailing edge of the central fin on wider boards, and is placed around the leading edge of the fin on narrower boards. For lighter wind and for working to windward, place a second back strap immediately in front of the first. If you're embedding webbing into the deck allow the width of your feet plus about three-quarters of a centimetre each side. If sinking threaded inserts into the board allow greater separation, say 16 to 18 cms between plugs. This also allows room for shoes.

Front straps You'll find two sets of front straps useful, one set for high speed, the other further forward for slower speeds.

From the rearmost strap insert of all, measure forward the width of your sailing stance to find the position of the corresponding front strap insert. Don't choose such a wide stance that you can't shift your weight behind the back foot while still in the straps.

Front straps are usually placed at 45° to the midline of the board and on narrow wave boards the set furthest back often share a common central insert. Place the second set of front straps 15 cm forward, locating each insert about 3 cm further from the board's midline to keep your heels clear of the first set.

SAILS Sails have altered dramatically during the last few years as designers have sought to make more efficient, more easily handled rigs. High-performance sails are taller and skinnier than traditional pinhead sails. Development towards the current shapes began when sails with high clews and shorter booms were developed in Hawaii for easier handling in high wind and to avoid dragging the boom end in the water when wave riding. As innovative designers like Barry Spanier of Maui Sails took area off the foot of the sail and reduced the distance from mast to clew, they transferred that area to the top where it has the potential to work more effectively. These tall skinny sails are known technically as high aspect ratio sails.

In gusts and when making sudden direction changes, the older low-tension sails tended to backwind (fill from the wrong side). Even when they didn't turn entirely inside-out, the power point or center of effort moved back drastically. To reduce this, designers increased rig tension by such devices as sewing more luff curve into the sail and using stiffer masts, using more seam tapes to tighten the edges, and using tensioned battens extending the entire width of the sail. We now have sails that can be set up with predefined aerofoil shapes even before the wind fills them out.

Klaus Simmer testing a sail designed by Barry Spanier for Dimitrije Milovich's wing-shaped rotational mast

Choosing a sail Choose your sail according to the type of board you'll use, the maneuvers you're likely to make, and the wind and water conditions. Ensure that you use a mast of compatible bending characteristics.

For the purpose of describing their characteristics, sails can conveniently be categorized into six broad types: General recreational, IYRU racing, Funboard course racing, Slalom, Wave, and Speed sails.

Funboard course racing sails are similar to IYRU-legal sails, but are made with fewer restrictions on dimensions and materials. They are fairly full compared with wave sails and fit longer booms. The sail extends down almost to the mastfoot, reducing the distance between board and sail. This enhances efficiency by slowing leakage of positive pressure from the sail's windward side under the foot to the negative pressure leeside – the so-called endplate effect. Masts should be very stiff, for example aluminum.

Slalom sails give a compromise between the power of course racing sails and the easy handling of wave sails. They are for radical maneuvers on small waves and relatively flat water. Flatter than course racing sails, with higher clews and shorter booms, they aren't as flat, high-clewed or short-boomed as sails made for riding large, consistent waves. Their masts should be more flexible than those for course racing, so they open more in gusts and the rider isn't overpowered during radical turns.

Pure wave sails need fairly stiff masts which are nevertheless flexible enough that the sail opens in gusts and the mast bends rather than breaks when a wave dumps on it. Aluminum is unsuitable because it kinks when bent. Epoxy fiberglass masts have suitable characteristics.

A wave sail needs less power than a flat-water sail, and power over a narrower range – though you need enough power to get out over waves, you don't want much power when surfing in. The ideal wave sail would be able to change shape, being fairly full when sailing out then becoming flat for surfing in.

Sail care The approved procedure for prolonging sail life is to wash in fresh water after each use, dry, then roll from top to bottom. Store in a lightproof bag. If you haven't room to store each sail without folding it, first fold it along its seams, then roll it lightly.

Designer Barry Spanier and ex-bushpilot Rick 'Sky' Kinser (right) working on a prototype

RIGGING UP

Boom height Some sailors like the boom between chin and eyebrow height, but it's a matter of personal preference and other sailors use lower booms. Bear in mind that a higher boom gives more leverage but less maneuverability.

Tensioning the rig A three or four-to-one pulley system on downhaul and outhaul will make it easier to achieve the tension required by many modern rigs. To get a good grip on the line you may need to wrap it around a bar, your harness spreader-bar for example. If you wet the rig before fully tensioning it, everything will tighten up better and you're less likely to have to stop sailing after 10 minutes to come ashore and take up slack.

It helps prolong the life of the sail if you tension the rig in stages, downhauling, then uphauling, then downhauling again, and so on. As tension increases, push your foot against the bottom of the mast and the boom end. The idea is to pull the downhaul until all horizontal wrinkles disappear from the sail, then increase outhaul tension until more horizontal wrinkles appear. Back to the downhaul: increase tension until the wrinkles disappear. Repeat until you have a taut, wing-shaped sail.

Batten tension is also important. Not enough and wrinkles run vertically to the batten. Too much and the batten becomes S-shaped. Fully battened sails with tapered battens that wrap around the mast to induce rotation require precise tensioning in order to function properly.

9 LAUNCHING & WATER-STARTING

CARRYING A SHORT BOARD AND RIG You can conveniently carry a short board and rig upwind and across the wind by carrying the sail on your head with the board upside down on top of the sail. The mast must be perpendicular to the wind or aligned with it so the sail flies.

To reach this position hold the mast in your windward hand and support the board with your leeward hand in a forward footstrap, palm up so that when you invert the board the hand is comfortably palm down. Lower your head into the foot of the sail and when you stand, taking the sail on your head, swing the board upside down onto the sail by crooking your elbow around the foot of the sail. Lay the board alongside the mast where you can hold it as you rest both hand and board on your head. Keep the windward rail tilted up so the board also flies.

One final tip: before lowering the board it's safest to walk knee deep into the water and well clear of rocks, because as you take the board off your head the weight shift tends to throw you off balance backwards.

LAUNCHING The way you launch depends on the particular circumstances. The beach start described here is ideal for a gently shelving beach.

Place the board into water of about knee height, just deep enough for the skeg not to ground when you jump on. Hold the boom with both hands in sailing position, sail luffing, and position the board on a beam to broad reach by pushing, pulling and levering on the boom. Control is easier if the board is against your leg, the mast step close to you, your rear leg just in front of the rear strap so you can easily place your foot on the board where it has most volume and will best support your weight.

Next, place your rear foot lightly on the board in front of the rear strap, using this foot for control as you sheet in. When you sheet in the board wants to head up, so keep it bearing away by tilting the rig forward or achieve the same effect by pulling the board back and under you with your rear foot.

As you sheet in fully, set the board in motion by pushing off with the foot still in contact with the bottom, making sure to keep your body weight and the rig's center of effort directly over the midline of the board.

All this is easy enough where there's little wave action. Launching in heavy beach break is more problematic and is described in the chapter on wave sailing.

WATER-STARTING The water-start is an energy-saving move in which the sail lifts you from the water, leaving you in sailing position fully-powered and underway. It's essential for sinkers and useful on any board to avoid exhausting yourself uphauling in strong wind.

Learning is relatively easy with a high aspect ratio sail, short boom and steady wind of 12 to 20 knots. Don't waste your energy trying to learn in light wind: the sail just won't pick you up, not till you've quite a lot of expertise anyway. Water-starting is also harder with a pinhead sail, full-length boom and sailboard fitted with non-retractable centerboard. The centerboard causes you to turn into the wind as the sail fills; the long boom weighs the sail down; while a pinhead sail doesn't have as much leverage to lift you as a fathead sail.

It's safest to learn on a board with enough buoyancy for easy uphauling should the need arise. Any centerboard should be fully retracted. On Maui newcomers to the sport often begin on sinkers and learn to water-start before learning to sail. I recall that board shaper Jimmy Lewis even sailed a sinker at Hookipa, the famous surf spot, before learning to gybe. He'd sail out through the waves to open water, fall in, turn the board, then water-start and surf in. I don't recommend you copy him, but this illustrates how water-starting increases your scope and safety.

TECHNIQUE

1 Practice in water shallow enough to stand in. Start with the board on a beam to broad reach and the mast perpendicular to the wind. I recommend you lay the boom on the tail of the board when you're learning. This lifts the mast from the water, making it easier to fill the luff with wind. You may have to slide the mast forward in its track for the boom to rest on the board. Positioning the mast forward also helps prevent the board turning towards the wind as the sail fills.

2 Tread water and catch wind in the luff of the sail by lifting the mast overhead and pulling it towards the wind in a sweeping arc. Speed sailor Fred Haywood, an excellent high performance coach, tells people to use the motion they'd use to pull the bed sheets over their head.

You can help stop the weight of the rig pushing you underwater by pushing down on the tail of the board with one hand or by reaching a foot under the sail and placing it on the board.

Downwind drift increases as wind catches the sail, so to maintain sufficient airflow you may need to resist this drift with several strong scissor or backstroke kicks while holding the mast overhead. Allow the sail to fill progressively as water drains off.

3 Pumping the sail slightly can help increase its lift. When it's clear of the water, transfer both hands to the boom (in moderate to strong wind) or place one hand on the boom and the other low down on the mast (in light to moderate wind) to increase the rig's leverage over your body.

4 With the board on a broad reach pull your body close to the board, knee bent up to your chest as Maui Meyer does in photo 4. This allows you to take some of your weight on the leg as you rise.

5 Sheet in hard to lift yourself clear of the water, pumping if necessary. In strong wind luff slightly as you reach a standing position, to avoid being catapulted forward.

Problems Board keeps heading up: lean the mast forward to bear off. Swimming forward also helps push the nose off the wind.

Boom end drags: lower the mast close to the water, letting the airflow lift the boom.

STARTING POSITION After a wipeout the board and rig are frequently aligned wrongly. The sail is often downwind of the board; the board may end up facing out to sea when you want to sail home; the clew may be facing the nose of the board.

Sail downwind of the board Short boards with short booms can easily be rotated around your body. Simply hold the boom in one hand, mast in the other, and lever the board around till it's downwind of the sail.

Provided you can gybe consistently it doesn't matter if this leaves the board pointing the wrong way. Water-start without delay, then gybe. This is often quicker than struggling to turn the board before water-starting. If your gybes aren't consistent you'll have to either turn the board or swim the sail around the board in the first place. Lead with the mast when you swim the sail around because the clew digs in.

Turning the board Short boards can be turned by pushing one end underwater and around under the sail. Long boards are more difficult to turn.

Flipping the sail When the clew faces the nose you'll have to fill the sail clew-first, then flip it over. Fill the sail by grasping the submerged side of the boom and pulling the clew towards and across the eye of the wind in a sweeping arc, catching air under the foot and the clew.

As the sail flips, slow it down by sliding your hand along the boom or, in really strong wind, by leaving the luff of the sail in the water. Otherwise the rig is driven underwater or gets so much momentum it flips several times or flies some distance away. Grasping the mast and pulling it towards you as the rig flips can also help leave the rig in ideal water-start position.

ADDITIONAL HINTS

Swells Swells can help lift you onto the board if you make your effort as the swell lifts you.

Strong wind Don't point the board on too low a heading in strong wind, because the force in the sail will be too great for a controlled start.

Light wind Once there's wind in the sail, placing your forward hand low down on the mast increases the rig's leverage over your body. The lighter the wind, the lower you place your hand. Keep your body beside the board, vertically under the rig. If necessary, place your entire leg over the board, heel hooked over the far side.

In extremely light wind put your rear hand on the foot of the sail instead of on the boom. Sheet in until the rig is upright, then lean the rig away from yourself slightly (to leeward), so its weight falling away pulls your body up. Meanwhile pull down through the mast to pull yourself up.

Gusts In gusty weather you sometimes pull yourself onto the board only to be catapulted forward by a sudden gust or dropped back by a lull. To avoid this, let go with your back hand the moment you're standing upright. Wait for the next gust, then sheet in.

Uphauling semi-sinkers When there's insufficient wind for water-starts you'll have to uphaul, so practice in safe conditions. Find the foot position which sinks nose and tail equally. Rocking the board from rail to rail with your ankles helps float the board up. In fact even full sinkers can be uphauled.

LANDING When launching you should have studied the beach so you know how steeply it shelves and where it's safe for your feet to hop off when landing.

Landing on a gently shelving beach is fairly easy providing you keep a safe distance from rocks and groynes and the currents they generate. Having unhooked the harness and taken your front foot out of its strap, sail in on a wave, staying on the broken whitewater as long as you can. When the water is knee deep, before your fin grounds, step off. Making your movements decisive, grip the mast in your windward hand, lift the board clear of the water with the other hand in the front strap, and get out of the water before the next wave arrives. With a board too heavy to lift out of the water, hold the back strap and push it.

On steeply shelving beaches with vicious shorebreak, land by following closely behind a big wave so you can sail some way up the beach on the surge. To get onto the back of a wave either catch up with it or, if you can do so safely, slow down and let the swell you're riding overtake you, then sheet in to keep up with it. Don't stay so close that you get caught in the crest as it breaks.

Problems Sometimes things go wrong and you find yourself standing in water too deep to pick up the board and run up the beach. Either hold the mast overhead to keep the sail out of the waves or, in water too deep for that, grab the mast near the top and push the sail underwater so waves pass over it rather than crashing into it. Having survived the first few surges you'll have to decide whether you can successfully wade ashore with the board or water-start quickly and sail a bit further.

Landing

Who says sinkers can't be uphauled?

10

GYBING

1

2

4

5

3

6

Once you can water start consistently you're ready to learn high-performance moves on a sinker or semi-sinker. Maneuvers such as the carve gybe and duck gybe are designed for planing speeds, so they bring into play forces different from moves at sub-planing speed on long boards.

Because of the higher speed, the effect of apparent wind – the wind created by the forward motion of the board – becomes significant.

Don't let the multiplicity of styles and technical variations for each maneuver deceive you into thinking its not worth making a detailed study of a particular rider's technique. Analyzing photos in order to work out the forces on a rider and on each part of his equipment can teach you an enormous amount. It also enables you to visualize moves before you do them, an essential part of smooth execution.

Carve Gybe A carve gybe is a smooth, arcing turn carried out at planing speed by sinking the lee rail. Ideally you emerge on the new tack without substantial loss of boat speed.

To carve a turn you bank into the turn. Bank to the left and the board turns to the left. Bank to the right, the board turns to the right. It's the board that causes you to turn, not the sail, though sail control also affects the speed and tightness of turn.

1 Initiate the gybe by bearing away to a broad reach, picking up as much speed as you can. On a broad reach you're normally leaning out but in this case bring your body upright, your weight over the board. A few pumps will increase your speed, making the board plane flatter, and also help pull your body upright.

Lean the mast forward slightly. Remove your back foot from the strap, placing the arch over the board's midline or slightly to leeward, wherever it's most comfortable to bank the board into the turn. You should bank smoothly and steadily throughout the turn.

2 Crouch as you enter the turn, to increase stability. Look through your sail window so you don't hit anything, and project a mental image of your course onto the water ahead, planning each stage of the gybe in advance.

3 At this point the sail is oversheeted and the rig feels virtually weightless.

4,5&6 The hull passes through the wind. Maui leans the rig well back before it can get power in it, placing both hands on the mast as the sail flips and pulling the mast across his chest to the windward side of the board. The sail flips around of its own accord if you're banking steadily through the turn. In fact, if the mast is leaned at precisely the correct angle it's possible to release both hands from the rig and let it stand free as it flips.

To reach the new sailing position, move your back foot forward while the front foot is still in its strap. The front foot is then pivoted and slid out of the strap so you can keep your weight bearing down on the board with both feet during the second half of the gybe in order to carve smoothly.

If, when you're learning, the board loses so much speed that it threatens to stall before you're powered up on the new tack, sail clew-first a short distance to regain momentum before flipping the sail.

Learning conditions You need sufficient wind to make your board plane throughout the turn. In marginal wind, pump to gain speed as you bear off. Flat water makes learning easier than rough water.

A short, light board loses less speed during the gybe than a long board, which makes technique for a 2.3-meter board somewhat different from a 3.4-meter board. If you have a centerboard it must be withdrawn or fully retracted before beginning.

Rough water If you're travelling very fast in rough water, slow down before gybing lest you hit a bump and bounce out. Learn to read the water and avoid gybing on the side of a chop that slopes opposite to the direction you're banking the board, otherwise you'll spin out. Select precisely where you turn, and bank the board against the side of a chop in the way a racing car corners on a banked track, so the chop aids turning.

Sail control On a short board you can gain so much speed while bearing off that as the tail turns through the eye of the wind your speed approaches that of the wind, making the rig feel almost weightless. During the turn there are several things you can do with the sail: (a) Trim for maximum drive, to emerge onto the new tack with minimum speed loss, (b) Oversheet, pulling the clew in towards the board and towards the eye of the wind, to facilitate a particularly tight turn, or (c) luff if overpowered.

In the illustration Maui Meyer uses the oversheeting technique. At the apex of his turn the clew is almost pointing into the eye of the true wind (frames 3, 4 and 5). While oversheeting he leans the mast aft towards the wind – two moves in one. Oversheeting serves initially to give a burst of power (like pumping), then it leaves the sail in neutral. Leaning the mast back stops it getting away or pulling you over when you let the sail flip around over the bow.

Duck Gybe To duck gybe you pass the sail overhead instead of flipping it around over the bow. This isn't a short board version of the old freestyle trick of throwing the sail onto the new tack and then gybing the board. It's a flowing sequence in which board and sail gybe together. The goal is to lose a minimum of speed, allowing the sail to luff only momentarily as you draw the clew through the eye of the wind.

As you bear off you need to gain more speed than for carve gybes because passing the sail overhead becomes much easier when apparent wind speed is zero or very nearly so. To achieve high boat speed you may have to pump quite a lot.

Just as for a carve gybe, remove your rear foot from the strap and use it to bank the board into the turn. Carve a smooth continuous turn. When you feel the sail lose power your speed is nearing that of the wind. Pull the sail in (oversheet) with your back hand, transfer the front hand back to within half a meter of the boom end, and then release with the other hand. Oversheeting serves first to pump, second to depower the sail by leaving it with clew pointing directly into the wind.

As you continue banking through the turn, pass the

1

boom in an arc overhead, through the eye of the wind, and at the same time pull the sail back towards your body. Reach for the new side of the boom quickly with the new front hand, before the sail gets power on the new tack. Ideally you should grasp slightly forward of the balance point of the boom. Place the rear hand on the boom as soon as you can.

Some people don't change foot position until they have both hands on the boom again, then they hop to the new position. Others, Robby Naish for example, switch foot position as they gybe the sail.

Incidentally, a duck gybe is a gybe in the purest sense, unlike gybes where you flip the sail over the nose, because both the tail of the board and the leech of the sail pass through the eye of the wind.

Troubleshooting A common problem is grasping the new side of the boom only to be pulled forward. This often happens when you grab the boom at its balance point and thus have the sail's full force to contend with. Try grasping it slightly further forward so you can let the clew swing out a bit, easing the pressure. Don't grasp too far forward though, because this allows the clew to fly around too much to leeward, spoiling the smooth flow of the sequence. And don't grab the boom behind its balance point or the mast won't swing towards you as you carve through the second part of the gybe. When learning, holding the foot of the sail as you go beneath it makes control easier beause you can hold close to the mast without the clew swinging around.

2

3

4

5

Maui Meyer duck gybes with one hand in the water

SNAP GYBE A snap or pivot gybe is much like a tail sink gybe on a long board. When snap gybing you lift the nose, lean the rig well to windward, and pivot the board swiftly on its tail by pushing with your back foot as you lever on the rig. The board virtually stops dead in the water and you emerge onto the new tack clew-first.

Unlike carve and duck gybes you don't seek to create a moment at the apex of the turn when the sail is depowered. In fact you want maximum power in the sail throughout, because when the board stops dead in the water you suspend most of your weight from the rig while your feet pivot the board.

Starting while planing on a beam reach, here's the sequence of actions in more detail.

First select a chop that will cross your path and plan to turn on that chop. This makes the gybe tighter and snappier because the chop pushes the board, acts as a ramp to lift the nose from the water and forces you to focus your actions into one clean, swift motion.

Head up to close hauled to slow down. This avoids popping your fins out of the water as you turn. As you meet the cross-chop, lift the nose of the board by throwing your weight over the back foot, back leg bent, front leg extended, leaning the rig to windward so you can lever against it to pivot the board on its tail.

Lean well back as the board turns through the eye of the wind because the sail will pull strongly as it becomes clew-first. Sail clew-first on the new tack just far enough to regain some momentum before flipping the sail around.

There's much arm and leg extension and contraction during this sequence, as the photos show, and you virtually sit down as the board pivots beneath you. It's great fun and not difficult. Even if your feet lose the board you can often complete the move by supporting your weight in the sail as you regain your footing.

TACKING Even a sinker can be tacked. For example you can ducktack and helicopter tack. To helicopter tack, turn the board past the eye of the wind, push the clew through the wind to sail clew-first on the new tack, then flip the sail over the bow into normal sailing.

11

WAVE SAILING

Photo John Severson

WAVES Most people surf and jump waves and chop generated by the local wind. These waves have short wavelengths (distance between peaks), steep faces, and tend to break irregularly. The big waves surfed in Hawaii and Australia, however, come from swells generated far out in the ocean. Ocean swells give the best surfing, forming long continuous peaks which break predictably.

When you're seeking surfing spots, look for beaches where the wind has travelled some distance over water. Wave height is related to fetch (distance from where the wave was generated), wind strength, and wind duration. Given a constant 30-knot wind, a fetch of 10 kilometers can give a wave of one meter, 30 kilometers a 2½-meter wave, and a fetch of 160 kilometers a 5-meter wave.

Wave type When a wave breaks over a gradually shelving bottom it gets higher and steeper until it breaks at the top in a tumbling, rolling fashion. This tumbling continues until the wave reaches either deeper water or the shore. Mushy rollers like these aren't too violent and are good to learn on.

A steeper shelf creates plunging waves. Plungers peak up very quickly, then break from top to bottom forming a tube. Because the entire force is expended in a moment they're particularly dangerous and should be avoided.

Wind on site also affects the way waves break. Offshore winds blow into the wave faces, making them stand higher and longer before breaking. Onshore winds tend to press waves down, making them mushy and making them break prematurely.

Study the waves you're going to ride before leaving shore. Get some idea of wave height, distance between waves and between sets. Notice whether the waves break to left or right or in both directions. A wave breaking from left to right of the person riding it is said to be breaking right.

For your first surfing experiences catch gently sloping swells and ride them until they begin to peak, then sail away from them. Stay away from shallow-water breaks and from waves that form tubes as they break.

WIND DIRECTION Waves break roughly parallel to the shoreline. Boardsailors distinguish five wind directions relative to waves. For your first experiences wind directions between 3 and 4, cross-shore to cross-onshore, are best and dead-onshore and dead-offshore are to be avoided. With more experience all directions except dead-offshore can be excellent, depending on factors such as wave size and type, wind strength and distance of the break from shore.

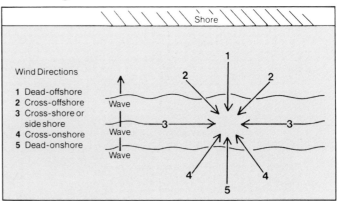

Shore

Wind Directions
1 Dead-offshore
2 Cross-offshore
3 Cross-shore or side shore
4 Cross-onshore
5 Dead-onshore

YOUR FIRST TIME For your first excursions select conditions carefully. Only surges should be hitting the beach, not breaking waves. The wind should be moderate, not too strong, blowing parallel to the shore or diagonally onshore. Ideally the waves should be rollers or spilling waves, definitely not plungers, with faces of one meter or less, breaking on a sandbar or reef at least 30 meters from shore.

LAUNCHING IN SHOREBREAK Two cardinal rules for shorebreak: One, keep your sail clear of the water, because once a wave dumps on it you'll probably lose control and quite possibly break some equipment. Two, never let the board become sideways on between your body and an oncoming wave or you may get hurt as the wave drives the board against you. A wave exerts tremendous force.

It's best to hold board and rig out of the water until ready to jump on and go, but if the board is in the water when a wave approaches, keep the nose pointing directly into the wave.

Waves tend to approach in sets. There'll be several waves close together, then a short pause before the next set. Observe the pattern so you can quickly place the board where there's sufficient depth for the skeg and set sail between waves. If you find yourself having to launch where all the waves are close together, don't stand around worrying how close each oncoming wave is. The split second a wave is past, jump aboard.

When placing the board into the water, remember that each wave increases the depth for a while. This means you shouldn't walk into water that's over your knees before a wave because when a waves comes the water will be up to your waist or higher. It also means you may be able to walk into ankle deep water, wait for a surge of whitewater, then launch in the deeper water behind it. That way you get the added advantage of sailing out with the momentum of the receding wave.

In time you'll learn the tricks of controlling the board in shorebreak. Take account of the forces of oncoming and receding waves and place the board a sufficient distance in front of you for a surge to bring it back.

As a wave approaches, turn the board to meet it head on by pushing away on the mast. Use the boom to lift the nose over the wave slightly.

If the surge returns the board to you sideways on, that's okay too, because you can turn it quickly by grabbing a footstrap or levering on mast and boom. And should a wave drive the board past you, keep the mast overhead and pull on it to pull the board back to you, keeping the mast perpendicular to the wind so you fly the sail rather than fight it.

SAILING OUT OVER SURGES AND PEAKS
Having jumped on the board you have several broken or peaking waves to negotiate before reaching open water, so bear away on a beam or broad reach to gain speed.

Approach each wave head on with plenty of speed. To go over waves the board should be planing. If you aren't planing, you're going through, not over.

In wind parallel to shore you can sail full speed directly at each face. In cross-onshore wind you'll have to sail the course shown below, heading up snappily to no more than close hauled in order to meet each wave as nearly head-on and with as much momentum as possible.

Sailing out in cross-onshore wind: head up snappily to meet each wave as nearly head on and with as much momentum as possible

Breaking Waves
Avoid reaching a wave just where it's breaking, and avoid walls of whitewater over one meter high. Look ahead to judge your course in good time, so you can head up or bear off to a less critical section. If that isn't possible, gybe and sail away from the wave – you'll have to be proficient at gybing!

Meeting the wave Ensure that your harness is unhooked. As you meet the wave, straighten your front leg and transfer just enough weight to the back foot for the bow to ride over the whitewater without the tail sinking in. The back foot can be in or out of the strap according to preference. Luff slightly on hitting the wave so the lurch doesn't throw you forward, then sheet in and push the board over the wave with your feet. Sheet out for an instant at the top if the board feels about to jump. Redistribute your weight evenly over both feet, and bear away to pick up speed for the next wave.

Weight the back foot to let the nose ride over the whitewater

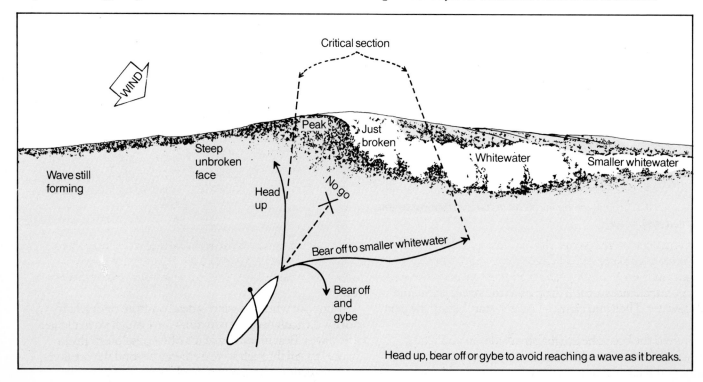

Head up, bear off or gybe to avoid reaching a wave as it breaks.

Sometimes it's difficult to stop the board becoming airborne as you mount a steep wave

If you fail to make it over cleanly but reach the top only to find you've expended all your momentum, luff and try to balance as the whitewater passes. Even if you drop the rig at this point, chances are it'll drop onto the swell behind the whitewater. Then you can safely water-start before the next wave.

Should the board be caught broadside-on you'll be knocked down or carried some way shoreward. On occasions you'll fall in front of a wave in water too deep for you to stand on the bottom and lift the sail clear. In these cases hold the mast tip towards the oncoming wave, board nearest land, and dive underwater, pulling the mast down as deeply as possible. Hang on tight and let the wave pass over you.

Sailing out when the wind is dead onshore or dead offshore is difficult because you don't have much power to get over waves. Bear in mind that it's often possible to find a channel to sail through so you emerge beyond the breakers, or some section where waves break at a more favorable angle to the wind.

WAVE RIDING Once you're beyond the breakers it's good to try a few gybes to loosen up and get used to the day's conditions. When ready, select your wave. The ability to identify waves that won't break early comes with experience. Riding the last wave of a set may be safest because if you wipe out you have more time to water-start before the next wave.

Catch your wave rather than letting it catch you. Head up to slow down, then bear off as it nears you, increasing your speed to match the wave's speed, pumping if necessary. As the wave lifts the back of the board, shift your weight forward to slide down the face. The apparent wind shifts towards the front as the wave increases your speed, so you need to sheet in more. To make sure you are indeed riding the wave, look along its length on both sides. When you've caught the wave you'll be able to sheet out and still be carried forward.

Once the wave begins to peak, start surfing back and forth along it by heading up and bearing off. Watch for rapidly steepening sections showing the wave is about to break, and get away by bearing off for extra speed. On a wave that breaks in sections and doesn't closeout (that is, all slam down at once) you can surf a section then move along as it breaks. Whenever the wave closes out, bear off and outsail it, sailing all the way to the beach if necessary. If it's possible to get far enough ahead and the whitewater isn't too fierce, gybe and gain enough momentum to punch through.

What not to do Avoid hanging on top of a cresting wave or you'll go over the falls.

Don't try to sail in whitewater because the skegs and rails don't grip well and the board slides or spins out.

While sailing back and forth on faces stay far enough from whitewater that it doesn't sneak under the board or burst under it lifting and tipping you.

Cutbacks You'll perform cutbacks naturally without having to be told how. Just so you know when you've done one, a cutback is a fast transition whereby after sailing up a face you turn the board at the top to go down again.

For example, you broad reach down a face and at the bottom turn into the wind enough to sail back up the face; at or near the top you cut back by quickly bearing off to sail down again.

RIGHT OF WAY ON WAVES These rules are derived from surfing, with additions for boardsailors. Following them will help avoid collision on the water and conflict ashore.

1 Swells aren't classed as waves.

2 The person (surfer, swimmer, board) taking off from the critical section of the wave peak has right of way.

3 Make your presence known to those on the same wave by shouting "Coming down".

4 The person coming in on a wave has right of way over the person going out through the sets, but each has responsibility to stay clear of the other.

5 When two sailors gybe simultaneously on a wave, the upwind rider has right of way unless the downwind rider is closest to the critical section.

6 In wipeouts and bailouts you must do all you can to avoid hitting others.

Right: Malte Simmer. Photo John Severson

Bottom turn followed by turn off the lip

TURNS OFF THE LIP You have considerable momentum as you complete the bottom turn and project yourself up towards the lip. Unsheet slightly to lose speed and shift weight from the lee rail to the windward rail without being pulled off balance. Slowing helps avoid cavitation and consequent spinout caused by a sudden transition from one rail to the other.

Off-the-lip turns are sharp turns made using both rail and rig. Initiate the turn by putting your back foot on the windward rail and weighting it slightly, turning the ankle to push down the back half of the windward rail. Simultaneously rake the mast back and sheet in to turn the nose. When sailing back down the face, bear off slightly to avoid going straight down and nosediving at the base. Leaning back slightly also helps prevent nosediving.

Bottom turns followed by turns off the lip aren't difficult in small waves. The trajectory of your bottom turn determines where you hit the lip, so look ahead to assess the wave in good time.

A true off-the-lip occurs at the critical part of a peak with the front part of the board visible from the back of the wave. Turns at the peak but not at the critical section are top turns. It's also possible to make aerial off-the-lips, getting airborne off the lip and turning in the air to land on the same wave.

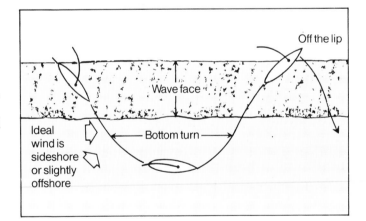

Robby Naish at Diamond Head

GYBING ON A WAVE Initiate the gybe by bearing off just before the wave. Sail up the face, continuing to bear off so that when you reach the top you're just passing through the eye of the wind. You'll be clew-first for a moment. Descend the face, flipping the clew around as soon as you can.

The technique is essentially the same as for carving a gybe on flat water except that (a) you plan the apex of the turn to coincide with the top of the wave (b) if you don't commit yourself to carving all the way around, or if your timing is off, you're liable to sail out onto the back of the wave (c) instead of slowing as you come out of the gybe you increase speed because you're surfing down the face, and (d) the board turns more easily on a wave, with less risk of spinout, because you're on a banked surface with the additional power of the wave.

*Richard Whyte makes a
low jump to maintain speed.
Photo Darrell Wong*

CHOP JUMPING Waves aren't essential for getting air-borne. Jumps can be made from completely smooth water given enough wind, though hopping off chops is easier.

First sail around and study the chop frequency. You may discover for example that every third or fourth chop has greater steepness and height. When you're ready to try a jump, sail on a broad reach to gain maximum speed. Then tighten up to about a beam reach, maintaining speed. Select the particular chop you'll use as a ramp, giving yourself about 7 meters lead-in. Keep both feet in the straps.

Aiming for your chosen ramp, bear away to a broad reach for an extra burst of speed, then just as you're about to hit the chop tighten up towards a beam reach again. As you hit, lift the front foot, pumping the sail, then quickly raise your back foot, pulling it up as close to your backside as possible. Pump the sail vigorously enough to encom-pass lifting both feet. Lift the windward rail slightly higher so the wind gets under it giving extra lift. Keep the sail sheeted in and leaning to windward for stability and vertical lift. Hang your weight down on the boom to sheet in. You'll notice that pulling in with the back foot and sheeting in tends to make the board turn downwind in the air.

Landing Don't look down. Look ahead and concentrate on continuing to sail on in a straight line as you land. For your first attempts don't try to alter board angle in any way. Simply remain sheeted as you were upon takeoff, and let the board land. This should give a tail-first landing. Flex your knees to take up the jolt. You'll have to make a con-scious effort to maintain mast angle because there's a ten-dency for the impact to make you pull it aft, which would make you turn suddenly.

WAVE JUMPING Different stages of wave formation have different steepness. A swell which hasn't yet formed into a wave has a smooth, gentle curve. As the wave forms its face progressively steepens until the wave peaks and then breaks. The steeper the face you project yourself off, the higher the jump.

For your first jumps pick the part of a wave that's forming and has a regular, moderately steep face, so your jump describes a low arc. Waves with regular one- or two-meter faces make good learning ramps. Cross-shore wind is best so you can sail perpendicularly towards the wave on a beam reach. In cross-onshore wind you'll have to gain plenty of speed on a beam reach, then head up perpendicular to the face at the last moment. It may be wisest to jump off the last wave of a set. Then if you fall you've a chance of getting back onto your board before the next set.

Though you need speed to project yourself into the air, don't build up so much speed that you feel unstable. Similarly, keep your sail adequately powered but be well able to control it upon takeoff. If you've a centerboard it must be fully retracted. The mast should be in its rearmost position. Keep both feet in the straps and as you prepare to meet the wave ensure your harness is unhooked.

Takeoff Sail directly up the face and continue sailing off the peak, keeping the sail sheeted in by hanging your weight down on the boom. For your first attempts don't push off or lift your feet as you leave the wave. Putting more weight on your back foot as you sail up the face creates a higher jump, as described later on, and for your first jumps it's best to stay low.

Throughout your flight maintain the angle the board had when it took off and you'll make a tail-first landing. If the board turns its nose towards the wind it's usually because you're pushing the tail away with your feet as you pull against the sail, when you ought to be holding your weight vertically down on the boom and pulling your back foot in beneath your buttocks. Pulling your back foot in also tends to raise the windward rail slightly, giving increased lift on the wind.

Landing Absorb the shock of landing by flexing your knees and, as for chop jumps, maintain the angle of the mast on impact. If you make a tail-first or flat landing, remain sheeted in and continue sailing. On landing nose-first, unsheet momentarily so the sail doesn't drive the nose underwater. Once the board is flat on the water again, sheet in.

Tail-first landings are easiest. Flat landings aren't advisable because they put enormous stress on equipment and your body, so if you look like coming in for a flat landing sheet out a little and extend your legs to drop the tail lower. Nose-first landings are least likely to break fins, but they're difficult to perform safely and should be avoided at first – if possible.

Bailing out If you lose control in the air, kick out of the footstraps and push board and rig away downwind.

CONTROL IN THE AIR Here are some hints on adjusting board angle during flight to achieve safe landings. In general it helps to think of yourself as sailing on the wind.

To lower the tail From stable flight it's possible to lower the tail by unsheeting, taking your weight off the sail, and also by extending your legs.

To lower the nose When you hang more weight on the sail the nose tends to drop. That's why you stay sheeted in for nose-first landings and unsheet for tail-first landings.

Controlling nosedives If you go into a nosedive its severity can be eased by taking pressure off the sail, raising the front foot, and extending the back leg. You can also control the nose by pushing the mast forward or pulling it back.

Turning from side to side Your direction of travel is largely determined at takeoff. Apart from mid-air acrobatics like donkey kicks, horizontal 360° spins and the like, you turn one way or the other in order to land with the hull aligned in the direction of travel.

Turn the board by holding your weight down on the boom while the front foot acts as a pivot between back foot and mast. For example, if the nose turns towards the wind, rotate it back onto the line of your trajectory by pulling your back leg in towards your body and pivoting the mast the opposite way.

LONG JUMPS To make a long jump, select a moderately steep ramp much like those for your early learning jumps. Gain as much speed as possible on approach. Then jump just before the board would launch itself, pulling the board upward by tucking your feet up under your backside and hanging your weight on the sail as described for chop jumping. This projects you into a long shallow arc.

As you near the water, either sheet out and drop your feet for a tail-first landing or let the board continue its trajectory and make a faster nose-first landing.

HIGH JUMPS To make a high jump, use a section of wave that's peaking steeply but not yet breaking. Approach with as much speed as you can. As you climb the face put extra weight on your back foot and use it to thrust off the top of the wave. This projects the board steeply into the air. At the highest part of your flight allow your weight to hang fully on the sail, causing the board to swing around under you and also slowing your descent.

Jenna de Rosnay. Photo John Severson

1

2

3

4

1

2

3

Back leg bent, almost sitting on the board, the rider's weight hanging on the sail causing the nose to drop

4

*Peter Cabrinha makes a flare jump. Thrusting his body sideways
as he leaves the wave, he hangs his upper body on the boom.
Photo Darrell Wong*

Funboard Racing 121

Funboard Racing 121

13

FUNBOARD RACING

World Cup racing
in San Francisco.
Photo WSMA / Cliff Webb

by Stefan Zotschew, Pool Manager, World Sailboard
Manufacturers' Association

Competitive boardsailing has two main directions: traditional Olympic-style triangle racing, adapted from yacht racing; and funboard racing with special courses and rules for competition in strong wind and surf.

Funboard courses and rules began developing in the late 1970s, notably with the Pan Am Cup in Hawaii. This was organized by the Kailua Bay Windsurfing Association and was a forerunner of the professional circuit.

In February 1983 the World Sailboard Manufacturers Association (WSMA) was founded to promote the interests of leading companies in the boardsailing business. This proved a major step forward for funboard racing because one of the WSMA's activities was to develop and run a funboard circuit. Accordingly the WSMA prepared a coherent set of tried and tested funboard racing rules, publishing their first rules book in March 1984. Among other things this book defined disciplines, courses, rights of way and scoring.

Slalom. Photo WSMA/Cliff Webb

THE DISCIPLINES A typical funboard regatta has three disciplines: course racing, slalom, and wave performance.

Course racing Funboard course racing differs from Olympic course racing in some important ways. First, the minimum wind speed required is an average of 15 knots over the course area. Second, the windward leg (beat) is relatively short – more than two-thirds of the course involves reaching, compared with an Olympic course which has 50 percent beat, 35 percent reach, 15 percent run. Third, the course involves many gybes.

This leads to a board design that is a compromise between maneuverability and speed on all courses. Length is typically 3.65 to 3.9 meters, width 60 to 65 centimeters. Sliding mast tracks are fitted and bottoms are double concave or a combination of double-concave in the front and single in the rear. Centerboards are fully retractable, 60 to 70 centimeters long.

Slalom This is held either as a figure-eight or a downwind slalom (sometimes called zigzag slalom). The start may be on the beach or on the water, depending on wind direction and beach conditions. As it's impracticable to start an entire fleet of 30, 40 or more boards at the same time, an elimination system is used. Heats often comprise eight or four contestants, selected by drawing lots, with four or two proceeding to the next round. In the WSMA World Cup the top eight or 16 contestants (according to the actual ranking list) are seeded in different heats so they don't meet until later rounds. Slalom boards are 2.4 to 2.9 meters long, with no daggerboard. Tail and bottom shapes allow high-speed, fully-controllable gybes. In some World Cups even top sailors have used stock production boards.

Slalom requires perfect water-starts in strong wind and in marginal wind, perfect gybes, and detailed knowledge of the rules. The event can be dangerous and great care must be exercised: imagine what could happen if the rider just in front of you fell and was hit by the nose of your board.

Wave performance This is the most loved and the most hated discipline. Riders don't win by passing a finishing line ahead of other contestants but must accept the subjective decision of judges. On the other hand the wave event is the most thrilling for riders, spectators and photographers.

A minimum windspeed of 12 knots is required. Duration of heats varies from five to 12 minutes depending on the number of contestants and the wind's anticipated reliability. As in slalom, entrants compete in heats with winners advancing to the next round and losers being eliminated (unless double elimination is required, rather than single). Only two sailors compete against each other in each heat, closely observed by a panel of at least three judges. The contestants are scored in three categories: jumps, rides, and transitions (radical maneuvers).

Boards used for wave performance can be the same as for slalom, but top sailors usually use special boards, including asymmetricals.

THE RIG Professional riders customarily bring at least 10 complete rigs to a regatta, using different rigs for different events and conditions. Few amateurs can afford so many sails, booms and masts, so their best strategy is to start with a few rigs, following the guidelines on the needs of each discipline given in the section on sails in chapter eight of this book.

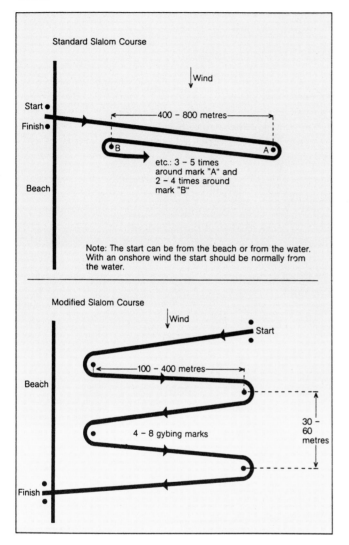

Standard Slalom Course

Wind

Start
Finish

400 – 800 metres

B   A

etc.: 3 – 5 times
around mark "A" and
2 – 4 times around
mark "B"

Beach

Note: The start can be from the beach or from the water. With an onshore wind the start should be normally from the water.

Modified Slalom Course

Wind

Start

Beach

100 – 400 metres

4 – 8 gybing marks

30 – 60 metres

Finish

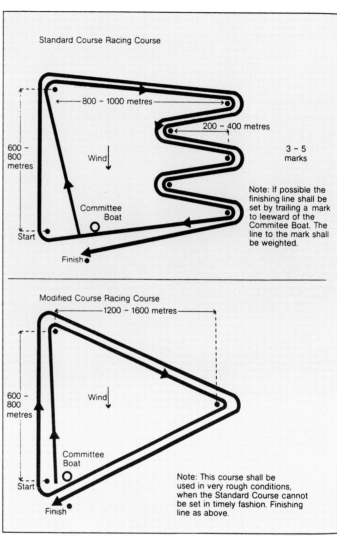

Standard Course Racing Course

800 – 1000 metres

200 – 400 metres

600 – 800 metres

Wind

3 – 5 marks

Committee Boat

Start

Finish

Note: If possible the finishing line shall be set by trailing a mark to leeward of the Commitee Boat. The line to the mark shall be weighted.

Modified Course Racing Course

1200 – 1600 metres

600 – 800 metres

Wind

Committee Boat

Start

Finish

Note: This course shall be used in very rough conditions, when the Standard Course cannot be set in timely fashion. Finishing line as above.

Fuerteventura. Photo by Ulli Seer. Used courtesy of HiFly

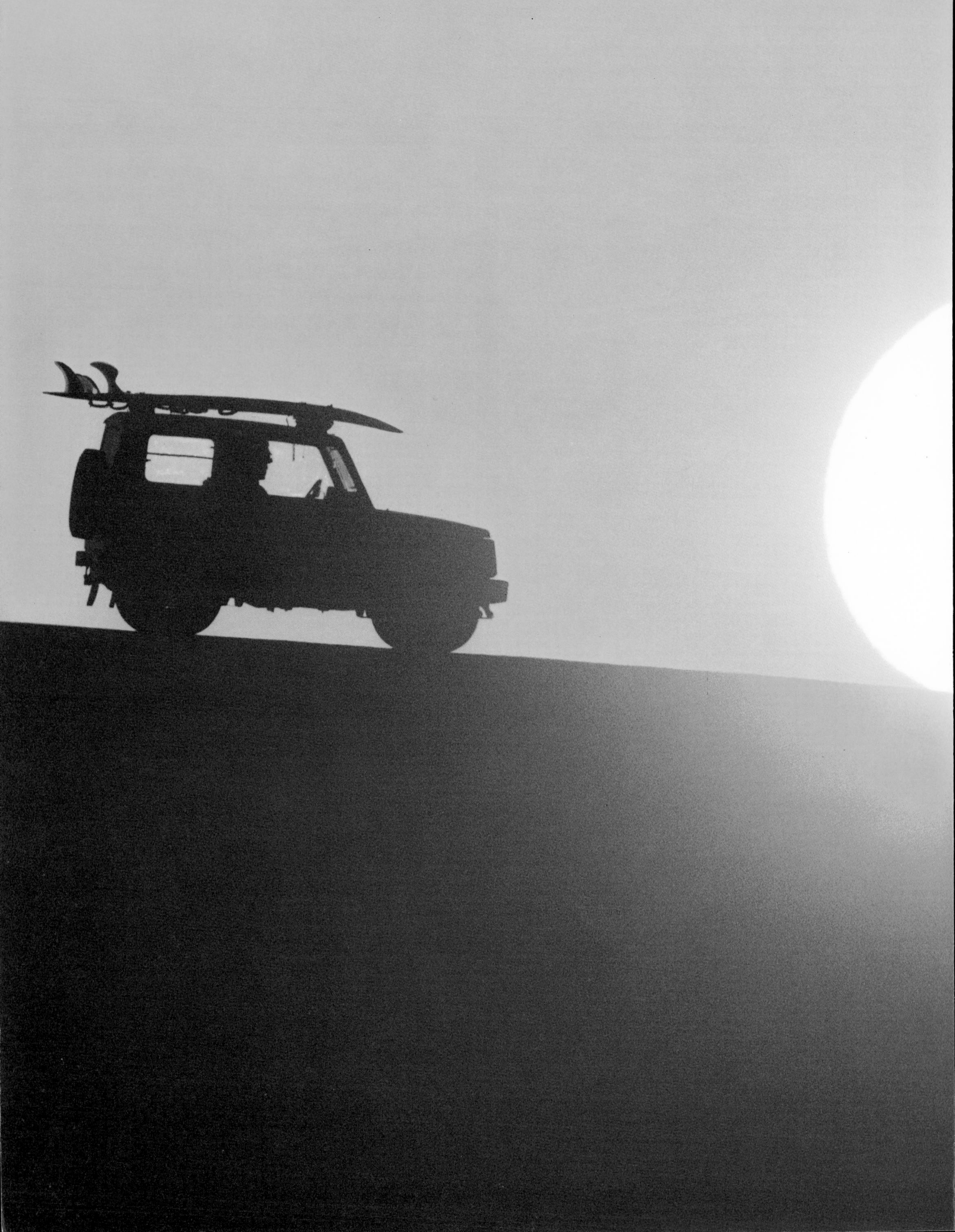

GLOSSARY

Abeam   at right angles to the centerline of the boat.

Aft   at, toward or near the stern or back of a boat.

Battens   flexible, removeable strips of plastic inserted into special pockets in the sail to give it shape.

Beam reach   sailing with wind abeam.

Bear off   (bear away): to alter course away from the wind (opp.—head up).

Beat   the windward leg of course.

Beating   sailing to windward close-hauled on alternate tacks.

Bow   the front end of a board or boat.

Broad Reach   sailing with wind abaft of the beam.

Center of effort (CE)   point through which all the aerodynamic forces on a sail may be imagined to act. All these forces are in balance at the CE.

Center of lateral resistance   point on the sailboard through which the resistance to sideways motion may be imagined to act.

Close-hauled   sailing as nearly as possible into the wind.

Close reach   point of sail between beam reach and close-hauled.

Eye of the wind   the direction from which the true wind is blowing.

Fore   at, toward or near the bow or front end of a boat.

Forward   forward part of boat, near bow.

Head to wind   headed directly into the wind.

Head up   to turn toward the wind (opp.—bear off).

Jibe (gybe)   to change tacks by turning away from the wind, change tacks with the wind aft.

Leeward   downwind.

Luff   (noun) the forward edge of a sail.
—(verb) (1) a sail luffs (U.K.: lifts) when wind strikes the leeward side of the sail ("back" of sail) near the luff. (2) to bring head to wind.

Luffing point   point at which sail just ceases to be completely full and starts to flutter.

Off the wind   any course other than close-hauled.

On the wind   close-hauled.

Pearl   a board pearls when the nose drops enough to dig in and slow or stop the board.

Port   left side of boat when looking forward.

Port tack   sailing course in which the booms are to starboard.

Rig   unit comprised of mast, sail, boom and mastfoot

Running   sailing before the wind.

Sheet in   pull in with back hand to harden sail (opp.—sheet out).

Starboard   right side of boat when looking forward.

Starboard tack   sailing course in which the booms are to port.

Stern   aft part of a boat.

Tack   (noun) the lower, forward corner of a sail.
(verb) (1) to work to windward by sailing on alternate courses, so the wind is first on one side of the boat, then on the other.
(2) to change tacks by turning head to wind (opp.—jibe).

Unsheet   sheet out; empty sail of wind by pushing away with back hand.

Weather   windward.

Windward   toward the direction from which the wind is coming (opp.—leeward).

Yacht   a general term for a vessel used exclusively for pleasure.

INDEX

Also by Roger Jones